1

AT HIDDEN LAKE

P.S. WINN

© 2015

This book is a work of fiction, names, places, characters and happenings are a work of the author's imagination. Any resemblance to people, places or actual happenings is purely coincidental.

Chapter 1

Looking out the passenger window of her friends' car, Andrea could see the sunlight as it streamed through the trees that lined the road. She closed her eyes a moment, thinking how much she really needed this three day weekend getaway. Lately her life seemed to be going in a downward spiral and she needing something uplifting to bring her out of that spin.

Never belonging to any specific religion, Andrea still considered herself a spiritual person. She had always been curious about religious aspects of life and whatever came before and after this life we all had to endure. That was also the word she would have used to describe her life, endure. It seemed all her life had been a struggle, beginning with the loss of both her parents when she was three years old.

Michael and Susan Larson had been killed
in an auto accident. As they had driven their
car on what should have been a short ride to
the airport. The couple had planned a trip to
California to meet with an investor in a
small jewelry company they had started. A
drunk driver, speeding through a red light,
had quickly and without remembering the
incident, due to his drunken stupor, taken
the couple out of this life and away from
their beloved daughter twenty four years
ago. Andrea barely remembered her parents,
if the recollections she had were even real
and not formed by the stories her
grandparents shared.
A wing shaped locket she wore around her
neck, held the picture that was almost her
only true memory of the two special people.
Her mother had made the locket and put in a
keepsake box for a young daughter she had
only known a few short years.

Luckily for Andrea, her grandparents, Martha and Gary Vanussa gladly took her in, after the tragedy. They had been the ones babysitting her that fateful day. The void and emptiness left by the loss of their daughter and son-in-law had been filled with the care of their beloved and only grandchild. The two tried to keep the memory of Andrea's parents alive through the retelling of stories and old photographs. Andrea was thankful to her grandparents for not only the recalled memories of her parents, but for the special ones she had shared with the couple.

Now, her grandfather was gone too. That's why Andrea was so grateful that her two best friends, Melanie Grayden and Seth Reynolds had invited her on this camping trip. It was Seth and his family who owned the small cabin here at Hidden Lake. Because Andrea had always considered the woods to be a spiritual place, she was also glad to be headed there right now, hoping

for closure in the newest tragedy that had
come into her life.

Andrea turned her head away from the
window, to look at Mel, her blue eyes
shimmering with unshed tears as she
dredged up memories usually kept tightly
snuggled in her heart.
"Thanks so much for driving me up here
Mel. I've been having a hard time losing my
grandpa and I know being up here is going
to help. I can remember Grandpa, grandma
and I coming up and camping in this area a
few times when I was a kid. We really had
fun."

Smiling at her friend, Mel nodded, her own
dark brown eyes also starting to tear up.
Being Andrea's best friend, she had spent a
lot of time at the home of Andrea's
grandparents, loving them both like they
were her own. "How is your Grandma doing
anyway? She must really miss your

Grandpa. Your grandparents were married a long time weren't they?"

Closing her eyes a moment, Andrea then smiled, her blue eyes now dancing with delight, thinking of her Grandma. "They were together for what seems like forever, but I really think she's doing terrific. You know, she was having a bad time at first. I think mostly it was being alone in that house with all the memories and with just her alone there now. I really feel she has come to terms with the fact that Grandpa is gone and is trying to go on with her life until she sees him again. In fact right now she is probably just getting off her flight back to Michigan. She went to spend some time with her sister."

Concentrating on her driving, Mel spoke without taking her eyes from the narrow road. "That's really cool, your Grandma is one special lady and I only wish the best for her. What makes her think she'll see your

Grandpa again? Is that what you believe will happen too?"

Andrea nodded, eyes wide. "Don't you think that way? I mean I guess we never really talked about it, but I just thought you did. Maybe because your mom is so religious, I figured you believed the same things she does." Turning to stare out the window, Andrea once again, absently fingered the necklace she wore. "My parents died when I was so young, I can't remember much about them and I have to think I will be reunited with them again. If I didn't believe that way, my parents' deaths and now grandpas' would be too hard to take." Andrea's head turned to look once again at her friend, wondering what she would think of the statement she had just made.

Mel only shrugged and shook her head of brown hair that was so dark, it looked black. When Melanie stood in the sun, the dark red highlights shone through. Something Mel hated. Her eyes, now narrowed as they looked at Andrea, turning almost as dark as her hair. "I don't know, I hope there is something more after we die, but I have no proof. I guess you just have to have faith. My mom does and she says there is. Then again, she thinks she sees angels everywhere."

As they pulled into the cabin that Seth had invited them to, both Andrea and Mel smiled at the sight of Seth's truck sitting beside the cabin and then stared around at the beautiful area. Sighing, Andrea turned back to Mel. "I'm not a hundred percent sure about what happens in the afterlife myself, but I do think we go to a better place. What if I didn't believe and on judgment day I got sent somewhere I didn't want to be just because of my non-belief?"

Mel laughed, the sound musical. "Andrea, you are too nice to end up in the wrong place. Never mind all of that right now, let's go see what Seth is up to."

Just as she said that, Seth came walking out of the cabin, smiling and waving. The two friends got out of the car and exchanged hugs with the big man. Both thanking him more than once for inviting them up for the long weekend. Seth shook his head of black hair. "The two of you don't need to thank me. I'm glad you both could come. Right now, just hurry and bring your things inside and let's worry about getting me some dinner."

As he said the words, Seth rubbed his stomach and the two women heard a loud grumbling sound.

Laughing, Andrea turned to Mel. "Did you hear that? We better hurry and dig this poor guy up some food before we start looking like dinner to him. He sounds like an angry grizzly bear."

The two followed Seth in the cabin through the kitchen door. Pointing toward the living room area where a couch and two chairs sat, Seth nodded toward the couch. "Just throw your bags on there, you can put your stuff away later."

After the bags were put down, Mel motioned toward the cupboards, before turning back to Seth. "Do you mind if I snoop around in the cupboards and see what you have stashed? Maybe I can come up with something to stop that awful noise your gut is making."

Lifting an arm, Seth moved it in a sweeping motion, his dark eyes dancing with humor. "Be my guest, what's mine is yours, just as long as it means I will be eating soon."

Seth leaned his six foot two inch frame back in the chair and crossed his legs. It wasn't hard to see that he was an athlete. Andrea and Mel both knew that Seth had been on his way to being a number one draft pick for the NFL when a skiing accident had messed up his knee and put a stop to his dreams of joining any football team.

When Mel walked over to take a look in the cupboards, Andrea joined her. The kitchen was small, but everything was in order, letting the woman know that Seth's mom, Gwen, probably did the organizing. Searching through the cupboards the two friends were delighted to find all the ingredients they needed to make what they hoped was not only a special, but a filling dinner.

A half an hour later the two had managed to put together a large pot of spaghetti and had it simmering on the stove, while they were attempting to make garlic bread in the cabin's tiny oven. Andrea turned to Seth frowning. "I didn't even ask how you have electricity in your cabin. I didn't see any power lines up in this area."

Seth smiled. "This place has its own generator. My dad put it in years ago. Before that we just camped the old fashioned way. The reason he bought the cabin was for the lake. My dad bought this place before I even started grade school. He didn't care much whether it had electricity or running water. He just wanted a good fishing spot, but my mom insisted on power, she was always more of a city girl."

Andrea laughed. "I'm with your mom, I like the woods, but I still am all for electricity. You can tell her thanks from me."

Mel nodded. "Me too, I don't think I could manage making spaghetti over a campfire, my specialty would be limited to roasted marshmallows."

Andrea pulled the bread from the oven, frowning at the loaf that seemed a bit twisted. "I'm sorry, this doesn't look all that enticing, but it does smells good."

Rubbing his hands together, Seth stood. "It is a lot better than what I could have come up with. I'll even do my part and grab some plates."

As soon as Seth grabbed mismatched plates from the cupboard, Mel grabbed cold beers from the refrigerator and the three sat down to their makeshift dinner.

Seth shoved the spaghetti and garlic bread in his mouth like it was his last dinner. Andrea and Mel exchanged glances. They both knew that Seth ate like this all the time and often. Andrea was always surprised Seth didn't weigh a lot more than his just over two hundred pounds the way he ate. She couldn't remember ever seeing him exercise in the four years she had known him. She and Mel had met Seth when Mel's older brother, Paul had brought him to a dinner at their mom's house. Seth and Paul attended college together at the time and played on the same football team. Both of the ladies had hit it off with Seth right away and it didn't take long for the three to become fast friends.

Andrea and Melanie had been friends since way back in junior high school. Andrea had been given an assignment in science class to dissect a frog. She had adamantly refused and the teacher had made her stand in front of the class and explain the reasons for her refusal. Mel had watched as Andrea had almost broken down into tears, hating to be the object of everyone's stares. Standing, Mel had walked up next to Andrea and joined the teenager in her protest of the project. Neither had many friends back then and after they had joined forces in the fight for frogs, they found they both had a lot in common with each other and not so much with the others in their class. They also found they liked it that way and mostly just hung out together.

When they met Seth, they found he had the same point of view as they did. The two also found Seth to be a bit of a loner in spite of his acclaim as a football hero, and they added him to their small circle of friends. After that, the trio were together all the time.

After dinner, the three cleaned up the mess. As the three worked together, laughter filled the air. Seth reached in the rinse water and splashed it on the two women, smiling and pretending it was an accident. Andrea finally threw the wash cloth she was using at Seth to get even. "Just because you're bigger than Mel or me, doesn't mean we are going to let you get away with any hijinks Seth."

Mel nodded. "That's right, if you want to make it two against one, just remember dynamite comes in small packages."

Seth held up his hands. "Okay, okay, I give, I know when I'm outnumbered. Let's call a truce."

The woman agreed and then grabbing another beer, the three went to sit on the deck that opened off the cabin's living room, through a sliding glass door. The wooden structure sat right on top of Hidden Lake.

Stepping out, Andrea took a deep breath of the fresh air. "This place is so amazing Seth. I am so thankful you brought us up here. I really needed some quiet time in a place like this, and the company of good friends. With Grandpa passing away, it brings up a lot of memories of other losses. Never mind about that though, I have it under control." Andrea frowned. "So, how come you never invited Mel and me up here before?"

Seth shrugged. "Usually someone else in the family is using the place. You've met my brothers, all Brady and Jarod talk about is hunting and fishing. They always seem to be grabbing this place before anyone else gets a chance. I was lucky to get this place and have it for the three days we all have off from work. Anyway, I wasn't sure the two of you liked the rugged life. Most women I know don't."

Mel laughed as she took a chair. "I really worry about you Seth, maybe you're hanging out with the wrong women. I'm with Andrea, this place is awesome."

Seth smiled as he took a seat and gestured for Andrea to take one also. "I'm glad you both like it. I do have to warn you about this place though."

Both women looked skeptically at Seth. Instead of taking the offered seat, Andrea shook her head. "No wait, let me guess. There was a murderer up here and his victims' bodies are buried around the lake somewhere and now their spirits are haunting this place."

Not waiting to hear an answer, Andrea instead turned from Seth and walked over to the railing on the cabin's deck. From where she stood, Andrea could look over the side and see straight down into the water. Smiling as a fish jumped just below her, making a loud splash on the waters' surface, Andrea finally turned away from the railing. Pushing back her shoulder length light brown hair from off her forehead, Andrea took a moment to stare at Seth. "Go ahead and tell your stories Seth, but I have to tell you I just can't believe anything bad could happen in this beautiful place. Not only is it amazing to look at, but it just feels so serene."

Seth again pointed at a chair and looked at Andrea, his face serious. "If you want to hear them, I think you better sit down. These stories are the type that are taken better if you are sitting down, not standing."

Rolling her eyes, Andrea walked over and took the chair. "Okay Seth, tell your stories, I'm all ears."

Seth looked from Andrea to Mel, who took a sip of beer and then nodded for Seth to go ahead.

Taking his own, much longer, drink of beer, Seth then began talking. "Both of you should know, there's more than one story and they aren't just folklore. A lot of people have seen some strange things up here at Hidden Lake. Maybe we should start back over a hundred years ago. I think it was around the time of the First World War. In fact, even before this story I'm about to tell, the town of Hagen Falls tragically must have lost at least half its' population to the fighting during that war. Back then, it was a farming community and not much else. The men and most of their sons, even those too young to fight, had gone off to do battle for their country."

Seth took another drink of his beer, making sure he had both his friends' attention before continuing. "Food was getting scarce and some of the women, most with young children to feed, headed up here to Hidden Lake. With the men gone, they didn't have money coming in and were living off what they could grow. They knew a supply of fish would go a long way in feeding their hungry families. I think it had to be around this time of year or maybe even a little later."

Andrea frowned. "What about what you just said about them being farmers, didn't they have their crops or fruit from the trees around here? You'd think September would be when their main harvest was."

Seth shrugged. "Who knows? Maybe it was a bad year for crops or even later in the season. All I know is they came up to the lake. I was told it was a group of a dozen women that made that journey up to Hidden Lake and sadly not one of them made it back to Hagen Falls."

Seth paused his story when he said those last words and watched as the two women's eyes widened before continuing. "After three days of waiting and worrying, another group, mostly ladies and the few teenagers who hadn't joined the war, came up here looking for the first group of women."

Seth pointed to the far side of the lake. "They found the women in a cave over there. This place is well known for its' abundance of caves. I'm sure many of them haven't been discovered even now. When the group got here, they looked around the cave and found the missing women, unfortunately none were alive. Body parts, bones and clothes had been strewn everywhere around the interior of the cave. A large pot was spotted sitting in the center of the area. It was filled with water and sitting on a fire that had almost gone out. One of the women walked over and looked in the pot, she almost fainted as she saw a hand floating in the murky water."

Seth took a deep breath, pausing a moment before he finished with the story. Andrea and Mel waited, afraid to interrupt their friends' strange tale. He watched them as they anxiously waited, giving them a few moments to think about the image he had created before he spoke again.

"The group left the cave, devastated at the loss and the horrific circumstances behind it. One of the women began giving orders to the others for a plan they had to carry out. When they finished the group hid and waited. A few hours later, a man, wearing what appeared to be animal hides walked into the cave. He was covered in blood and dirt and when he stepped in the entrance, he didn't even bother to search for witnesses to his repugnant acts. The women and teenagers followed him in the cave and using the meager weapons of rocks and sticks they had been able to gather in the woods, beat the man to death."

Mel gasped and covered her mouth with her hands. "Oh no, how terrible. Did they ever find out who the guy was?"

Seth shook his head. "If they did, I never heard about it, but sometimes at night, people say they can hear the cries of that first group of women he killed and was eating. So, if you find yourselves outside at night alone, just be careful."

Frowning, Andrea shook her head. "I can tell you with all certainty, I don't plan on being alone. What an awful story Seth." Then she stared at him, her blue eyes curious. "Have you heard them?"

The wide shoulders lifted in a shrug. "I don't know for sure. My brother's and I have spent a lot of time up here and have explored all over this area. We've been in dozens of caves. I've heard noises, but I have always made myself believe it was nothing more than the sound of the wind." Seth grinned at Andrea before turning and sharing the smile with Mel. "Maybe the two of you will be lucky enough to hear the sounds while you are up here. Then you can tell me what you think."

Andrea shook her head. "I wouldn't call that luck. Thanks a lot Seth, now every noise I hear is going to freak me out."

Mel nodded. "That goes double for me. If I do hear anything, I'll be running straight to your room for help Seth."

Seth laughed. "At least the two of you are going to be sharing a room. You can protect each other. I'll be all alone in my room."

Andrea laughed. "Hey, just call that payback for telling us that awful story. Besides you're twice as big as either of us."

Seth held up his hands. "Come on, don't be mad, I just thought you both would want be prepared. Does that mean you don't want to hear anymore?"

Andrea was about to say she'd heard enough when Mel interrupted her. "I want to hear the others. There's one in particular I'd like to know about. I heard my mom talking about a UFO being sighted up here and some strange lights people have seen too. Do you know anything about those?"

Andrea nodded then. "Hearing that story would be a lot better than hearing about a murderer and cannibal."

Leaning back in his chair and taking another drink, Seth nodded. "There have been a lot of unusual sightings up here. I'd say most of them involve strange lights in the sky." Seth pointed at Mel. "I think what you heard your mom talking about was probably what happened back in the seventies. She couldn't have been very old though."

Mel tilted her head thinking. "My mom was born in sixty six, so she was young. Even if it was the late seventies, she probably wasn't even a teenager at the time it happened."

Seth nodded. "From what I've been told, the big sighting was in the seventies when a group of boy scouts came up here on a camping trip. They were out studying the stars as part of a scouting project and thought they saw a spacecraft in the sky. Following its' path, they said it landed on top of a hill. In fact it wasn't too far from the cave where the murderer was killed. You know how people are, they mostly dismissed what the kids said, but even today if you go over to that hill and hike up on top, you can see this flat space that looks almost like it could be a landing area. It's overgrown now, but you can still see the spot that looks like at one time someone cleared an area right on top of the hill."

Staring wide eyed at Seth, Andrea smiled. "Wow, I'd really love a chance to see that."

Seth laughed. "I thought you might. I already planned on taking the two of you up to see it tomorrow. We can pack a lunch and hike up there. It's only about a mile away from here."

Mel pointed at Seth. "I think you're probably more interested in the lunch than the hike."

Seth finished his beer and smiled. "You might be right about that. I have to tell you both though, I've been up there at least a hundred times and I can only remember seeing something strange once."

Both Mel and Andrea stared at Seth. He had to smile at the anxious looks on their faces. "Don't get excited. I just thought I saw some colored lights above that hill. They vanished so quickly, I think I must have imagined it. That same night though, on the way back to the cabin, I found a strange looking gold necklace outside a cave that's not too far from that hill. For weeks after that, my family and I hunted around but never found any more of what I was convinced had to be a hidden treasure. In fact my brothers and I made a game of it. You know how kids are. We became treasure hunters who were going to become famous for the amazing treasure we uncovered. We never did become legendary for that, but my dad and brothers said they have seen the lights more than once. For me, unfortunately, that was the one and only time."

Andrea frowned. "Do you still have the necklace?"

Seth nodded. "Yeah, it's back at my place in town. I did have it looked at once, by a guy I knew who had a bit of experience with that kind of thing, he told me the necklace was probably made in the late thirties or early forties and is twenty four carat gold. He said it was worth a lot, apparently because it has a quite unique design."

Andrea's eyes grew large. "That's so cool, can we see that hill from here? I mean it's starting to get dark, maybe we could get a glimpse of those lights."

Seth shook his head. "Sorry, there's too many trees and other hills in the way." Seth slapped at his arm. "Besides, we need to get inside. The mosquitoes will eat you alive out here. They're really bad because of the water." Seth stood up. "C'mon, I'll show you two where you'll be sleeping."

Andrea and Mel followed Seth back into the cabin where they grabbed their bags before following Seth through the small house. The place only had two bedrooms, one of which Seth stepped in ahead of the pair and spread out his arms. "This is your room for the long weekend, it's not glamorous, but at least the bathroom is right next door."

Just grateful for an indoor bathroom, Mel and Andrea took turns changing into their pajama's before they joined Seth back out at the kitchen table.

Seth smiled at both of the women. "A lot of men would be jealous of me right now. Alone in a remote cabin in the woods, with two beautiful women and in their pajamas no less."

Andrea laughed. "Good thing you're just like a big brother to me then."

Reaching over, Mel placed a hand on Seth's arm. "The same goes for me. Besides, whether you say we are beautiful or not, I have a feeling we're not your type. Which is okay with me, I love having you for a friend."

Seth shrugged. "To tell you the truth, I don't think I have a type. I turned thirty not that long ago and have never had a serious relationship. First, I was so focused on wanting to play professional football that I didn't have time for anything else. When that dream fell through, I was too bitter to care about much of anything. After that, I was lucky enough to land the job at the auto shop. I was so busy learning how to fix cars, I couldn't think of anything but that."

Andrea smiled. "I never saw you play football, but you are so good at what you do now. You're like an artist with what you can do to a car."

Seth shrugged, he didn't know if he was good or not. What mattered and what he loved was taking what looked like a piece of junk and restoring it to the classic car it once had been. The money was good too. All that really counted was the end product and that was what brought him satisfaction and a feeling of accomplishment. "I do like my job, but I still can't seem to find time for a relationship."

Mel laughed. "Hey, wait a minute, Andrea and I are both twenty seven and neither of us are in a relationship either."

Thinking that it was kind of sad that all three of them seemed to be in the same boat Andrea nodded her head. "I think I have too much baggage for a relationship. Look at me, my parents died tragically when I was a child. I was raised by my grandparents, who were pretty old fashioned in their ways. I don't think a lot of people understood me and thought I was different because I didn't want to join in their groups or go out partying. I just was never the popular type and to tell you the truth, I really never wanted to be. Most people only seemed to feel sorry for me and never bothered to take the time to really get to know me."

Andrea pointed at Mel and Seth. "Present company excluded of course. You two accepted me for who I am and neither of you looked like you might start crying every time you saw me. I hate pity and don't want someone to be my friend just because they feel sorry for me."

Mel nodded. "I know what you mean. I never lost my parents or anything like that, but with my mom being from Puerto Rico and my dad this big, blue eyed blonde with an eastern accent, people always looked at me like I was some kind of strange specimen."

Seth laughed. "That's so funny you said that. When your brother brought me to your house that first time, I have to admit I was a little surprised myself."

Mel frowned. "Oh wow, I never even thought about that. I guess Paul does look just like my dad." Mel smiled, thinking about the two men, both so different than her and her sisters.

Seth nodded. "Yeah, and he never mentioned the fact that his mom and two sisters were all at least a foot shorter than he was."

Andrea laughed. "And they are definitely not blonde haired and blue eyed. Mel, Olivia and her mom look like they could be triplets."

Seth nodded. "I love your mom though. For a five foot tall woman, she has a ten foot tall heart. Maria seems to love the whole world."

Mel shook her head. "You just haven't seen her when her temper come out. Believe me, she can fight with the best of them, especially when someone picks on her kids or her beliefs. She's deeply religious. I think that might have a lot to do with that big heart of hers. She believes in seeing the best in people, no matter how hard she has to look to find it."

Seth nodded and then yawned. "I don't know about you two, I'd love to sit up and talk all night, but I'm beat. It's strange how that always happens to me in the woods. I get tired early, but then I tend to get up at

the break of dawn."
He turned to look at Mel. "I hope you don't
think I meant anything bad about you being
so different from your brother."
Seth held out an arm and rubbed it.
"Since I am darker than you, I definitely
know what it's like being different."

Andrea shook her head. "Listen to you two."
Lifting a strand of hair, much lighter in color
than her friends, Andrea shook it. "In this
group, I'm the one who's the oddball. Now,
let's forget about all of that nonsense and get
to bed. I feel like Seth does, getting some
sleep sounds like a great idea."

Andrea leaned over and kissed Seth's cheek.
"Thanks so much for inviting me up here. In
spite of your crazy stories, I still feel that
being up here is going to be good for me.
The woods always feel so spiritual and
relaxing to me. That's just what I needed
right now. I already feel better and if we get
to see anything supernatural I will be in
seventh heaven."

Laughing at Andrea's proclamation, Mel stood and stretched, covering a yawn. "What I need is some sleep and that will be like heaven to me."

Leaning down, she also kissed Seth's cheek. "Sweet dreams Seth. See you in the morning."

Andrea and Mel headed for the bedroom they'd be using for the next few days. Behind them, Seth sat at the table smiling. He was so glad they had all been able to get together for this three day weekend. He'd known Andrea had been affected a lot more than she was showing by her grandfather's death. He really hoped tomorrow he would be able to share something special with both of his friends.

In the bedroom, Mel and Andrea got comfortable in the rooms' only bed. They pulled the thick blanket up to cover themselves. It was more of a patchwork quilt and Andrea wondered if someone in Seth's family had made it. Snuggling further under the blanket, Andrea stared up at the ceiling, waiting for her eyes to adjust to the darkness. When she spoke, her voice came out in a whisper. "I don't know if I'm more excited or afraid to take that hike tomorrow."

Mel smiled. "I think it will be great, and I could really use the exercise."

Andrea slapped at her friend's arm. "Melanie, you do not. I wish I was built like you. I look like a boy standing next to you. Believe me Mel, you have everything and it is sitting in the right places. You definitely don't need exercise."

Mel laughed. "Maybe, but I still think I could stand to lose ten or twenty pounds. Never mind that, besides the hike, I'm excited to see this place Seth told us about. I can remember the wonder in my mom's voice when she talked about the story. She didn't think the object people thought they saw was a UFO. My mom thought it was more like one of God's chariots. She thinks ghosts are angels and aliens came from heaven too."

Andrea turned her head and looked over at Melanie. "I love that idea. It makes the thought of ghosts and aliens a hell of a lot less scary. Maybe with that vision in my head, I can sleep without nightmares from listening to Seth and his stories."

Mel frowned in the dark. "Do you really think that story about the murderer being up here is true?"

Andrea sighed. "I think it probably is close to the truth anyway. Going back in history I know there are a lot of tales similar to that one. Our generation isn't the only one that has to deal with serial killers. Sadly, they were around back then too. I'd rather focus on the other story. How cool would it be to see a spaceship that came all the way from another world?"

With that thought, both Andrea and Mel slid into sleep.

Chapter 2

Andrea woke before Mel the next morning. The smell of coffee mixed with the enticing aroma of bacon had her slipping quickly and quietly out of bed. Leaving behind a soundly sleeping Melanie, Andrea headed first to the bathroom and then into the kitchen.

Turning as Andrea entered the room, Seth couldn't help the big grin that covered his face. Andrea's light brown hair was a jumbled mess and the yawn on her face made her look just like a small child on Christmas morning. One who was eager to see what was happening even though not quite awake yet. "Good morning sleepy head. Coffee is on and our breakfast is almost ready. Where's Melanie?"

Andrea pointed toward the bedroom. "Still getting her beauty sleep I guess. With these wonderful smells in the air, I don't think that will last long though."

Seth laughed. "Good, we need to eat, pack up, and head out. We've got a big day ahead of us. There's cups in the cupboard above the coffee pot. Grab yourself one and pour yourself a cup of coffee. There's cream in the fridge and sugar on the table. I'll just dish up this food, then I'll go and try to get Mel out of bed."

As Seth turned away from Andrea, he saw Mel coming out of the bedroom. As she headed toward the kitchen, Mel finger combed her dark hair. "I'm out of bed Seth. Who in the world could sleep with all the noise you two are making anyway?"
A smile lit her face. "Of course, those good smells might have something to do with my getting up too. Hey, I didn't know you could cook Seth."

Putting bacon and eggs on the plates, Seth laughed. "It's nothing fancy, believe me, but it should be filling. Grab some coffee and let's get this day started. I have to admit, the smells in here are even making me hungry."

As the two women sat down, Andrea shook her head. "Who are you kidding, everything makes you hungry Seth."

A shy smile crossed Seth's face, making him look half his age. Then, ignoring the comment, he sat down himself and began shoveling in the bacon and eggs.

Mel shook her head as she began eating. After the first bite, she smiled. "Since you aren't even taking the time to chew your food long enough to taste it and enjoy your own cooking, I'm happy to let you know it really tastes great."

After her own first bite, Andrea nodded. "It's surprisingly good Seth, thanks."

Seth answered between bites. "Just don't get used to it. I do my best cooking in the woods. Maybe it's the atmosphere, but food has always tasted better to me up here. At home I usually can cook up a fairly good hamburger, but not too much else. I usually stick to the microwave for most of my meals."

After breakfast and cleaning up, the three worked together to fix and then pack their lunches, placing the food in three backpacks that Seth had dug out of a closet.

Slipping on their packs, the trio left the cabin and with Seth in the lead, and began their hike.

As they walked, Seth pointed out several areas he knew would be of interest to the women. Mostly places him and his brothers had spent time as kids. It seemed almost every tree or bush held a special memory for Seth. Andrea envied both of her friends getting to grow up with siblings. She knew as an only child she had missed out on a lot, but then again she also had gotten one on one attention from both her grandparents and knew others might be jealous of that special relationship she enjoyed.

Andrea's musings stopped when a short time later they made their way to what Seth called Miners' rock. The thing stood at least eight feet high and was dark gray in color. Several names had somehow been cut into the hard surface.

Andrea stepped closer and ran a finger reverently over one of the names. She frowned as she turned back to look at Seth. "Who did this?"

Stepping forward, Seth and Melanie both touched the etchings. Seth looked at first Andrea and then at Mel as he explained. "It happened a long time ago. Back when Hagen Falls was first becoming a town. People had come west looking for a better life and decided to settle here. They cut trees and moved rocks from this area down to Hagen Falls to build their homesteads." Seth shook his head in wonder. "They must have had a regular rock quarry going on up here. Anyway, they left this rock here and those who had done the hard work, carved their names in the surface and left their mark behind."

Andrea stared in awe. "This is so beautiful, and what a great testament to those people. I can't even imagine how hard that must have been. Loading trees and rocks on wagons that were pulled by horses and then hauling everything back to town. Not to mention that after getting it down there, they still had to build a town. Those people were made of some tough material alright."

Both Seth and Mel nodded their agreement with Andrea's words. Mel then frowned. "I can't believe I never saw this before. I can't remember ever hearing any stories about it either and I've heard quite a few tales about this place."

Andrea nodded at that. "Mel's right, that is kind of funny. I mean I've camped up here with my grandparents. It's been years ago, but you'd think I would have seen this or heard about it."

Seth shook his head. "You both probably camped on the other side of the lake. That's where the campground is and where most people stay."

Andrea shrugged. "I guess so, it doesn't really matter, I'm just glad you're sharing it with us now."

Seth pointed at a faded pathway, lined with pine trees and overgrown with weeds and grass. "We better get going. The hill you want to see is over that way."

Reluctantly, Andrea and Mel stepped away from Miners' Rock and followed behind Seth. It took another half an hour of hiking before they could finally see the place that Seth had called a hill. To Andrea it looked more like a mountain. "Wow, that thing is huge."

Seth laughed. "Compared to a lot of the others places around here it's not. Most of the mountains in this area are filled with caves too. If the two of you are up to it, we can hike on up to the top."

Seeing the two look up at the large hill and frowning, Seth smiled. "Don't worry, there's a trail that leads up on the side. It looks tall, but the hike isn't too bad. When we get to the top, you can see the flat meadow. That's where people claim the UFO landed."

Both Mel and Andrea nodded excitedly, wanting to see the area they might be a landing field for something from outer space overrode any worries they had about a difficult hike. Seth took the lead and then continued up the trail with both women sticking close behind him. Hearing a loud noise, Seth stopped in his tracks. Turning back to the others, he frowned. "Do you two hear that?"

Andrea's face scrunched as she listened to what sounded like an engine running. "I do hear something, what is that?"

Seth shrugged. "It sounds like a large truck, maybe a dump truck or something like that, but it shouldn't be up here. This is a National Forest and protected. Once in a while they come up here, just to thin out the trees or something like that, but they always put a notice in the paper or on the news. I would have read about it. Whatever's making that noise, it can't be too far ahead. I think we should go take a look and see what's going on."

Seth had only taken a couple of steps, the two women close behind him, when all three were startled as a man stepped out from the bushes holding a rifle. The blonde haired man was almost as big as Seth and he had a scowl on his face. "This area is closed off.

Only authorized personnel are allowed in. You three are going to have to turn around and head back the way you came in."

Seth shook his head. "Wait a minute, this is National Forest Land, and we're allowed to be up here. This place is always open to the public."

The man lifted his gun slightly. The barrel wasn't pointed directly at Seth, but it was close enough. Taking a step back, Seth held his hands out to show they were empty. "We don't want any trouble. What's going on up here anyway?"

Shaking his head, the man motioned with his rifle toward the path behind the three friends. "That information is on a need to know basis and you don't need to know. Unless you want to be arrested, I suggest the three of you just turn around."

Seth turned to look at Mel and Andrea. "I think we better go. I don't know what's happening, but I don't feel like getting arrested either."

The women nodded, although neither of them felt right about the guy or the orders he was giving. They also knew right now, they didn't have much of a choice. The three turned around and walked back to the large carved rock they had seen earlier before they finally stopped.

Melanie shook her head. "What the hell was that all about? An armed guard, that's got to be a joke right?"

Seth's dark eyes filled with anger. "I don't know, but no one except the Forest Service has the right to be working up here. They definitely have no reason to have an armed guard standing on a public hiking trail and keeping people out."

Andrea frowned. "What do you think they're really doing up here Seth?"

Seth gave her a lopsided grin. "I don't know what's going on or why, but I do know one thing, I'm damn sure going to find out."

Both Andrea and Mel stared wide eyed at Seth. Melanie spoke first, but Andrea had been about to ask him the same question. "How in the world are you going to do that? You heard what that guy said, no one's going to be allowed in there. On top of that he was holding a gun."

Seth laughed. "Oh, I'll find a way in. You two don't have to go with me. You can stay at the cabin. You saw that guy. I'm sure there's more like him around. It might be dangerous."

Andrea shook her head. "I want to go with you Seth. I really don't like the idea of someone holding a gun on me. Besides, now I'm dying to know what's actually going on up here. There's no way you're leaving me behind at the cabin."

Mel's head bobbed in agreement. "I'm coming too. I feel just like Andrea, no way are you leaving me behind at the cabin and out of this adventure either."

Seth sighed. "Why did I know you both would feel that way?"

Looking at the two women Seth finally nodded. "Okay, let's head on back to the cabin. We need to come up with some kind of a plan. We definitely need to think of some way to defend ourselves."

Seth lifted his wrist to look at his watch. "On top of that, it's almost lunch time. I guess we can have the lunches we made back at the cabin. I wanted to eat on the plateau on top of the hill. Looks like our plans have changed."

Andrea and Mel both shook their heads as once again it seemed Seth's focus seemed to be on food.

Chapter 3

After leaving the trail, Andrea and Mel were seated at the table in the cabin, both were watching Seth. He had left them inside earlier while he had gone out and searched through a shed behind the cabin. When he came back, he brought several small canisters into the cabin with him.

Andrea frowned at him now. "What's in those containers Seth? You're not building a bomb or something are you? I want to find out what's happening on that hill, but I don't think we should hurt anyone."

Seth lifted one of the canisters. "We're not hurting anyone, but you can bet they would hurt us and not think twice about it. We have to be able to defend ourselves though, this is the best thing I could come up with."

Staring at Seth, Andrea shook her head. "That guy had a rifle Seth. I want to take a look up on that hill as bad as anyone does, but I don't plan on playing war with whoever's up there."

Holding one container up so Andrea and Mel could look at it, Seth smiled. "Don't worry, I'm not planning on starting a war. This stuff is only bear spray. It might be useful if I come face to face with someone pointing a gun at us again. The spray won't kill anyone, but it will put them off guard long enough for me to get that rifle away from them. I don't know if either of you have ever seen anyone after they've been sprayed by this stuff, but believe me, after they get hit with it, they won't be feeling like putting up a fight."

Seth looked at the two women. "That reminds me, I also have pocket knives for each of us."

Seth pulled open a drawer and searched around in it a moment before grabbing out three folded knives. Stepping over to the table, he handed one to Andrea and the other to Mel.

As they took the knives, both women had concerned looks on their faces as they wondered what in the world they were getting themselves into.
Mel stared at Seth when she took the small knife. "I hope you don't expect me to stab someone. I'm only five foot two, I don't think I could hold my own in a fight with a guy your size."

Nodding at Melanie's words, Andrea looked at her knife. "She's right Seth, I'm not much bigger than Mel. Even if I was a lot bigger, I think I might have a problem actually stabbing someone."

Mel laughed. "You're not bigger than me at all Andrea. You might be an inch taller, but you're twenty pounds lighter. I'm with Andrea though, I might not be able to attack someone."

Seth thought they both might find it a lot easier than they thought if they were threatened and had to fight back, but he shook his head. "I don't think either of you has to worry about anything like that. I just want us to be prepared. I'm not expecting any trouble. I just want to try and get a look at whatever it is they are doing up there."

Seth walked over to where their backpacks were sitting on the floor. Picking them up, he carried them to the table and began placing the few items inside. "We have binoculars, the bear spray and those knives. Unfortunately, we don't have much else. If anything happens, and I'm sure it won't, we'll have to rely on our own quick thinking more than anything else."

Andrea grabbed one of the packs and looked inside at the skimpy contents as she threw the knife inside to join the other things. "I'm not sure about all of this Seth."

Grabbing her pack, Mel nodded. "I'm with Andrea. We don't seemed prepared for anything except some bird watching or maybe scaring off a bear or two if we're lucky."

Seth's dark eyes narrowed. "I know this whole thing sounds crazy. I can't help myself though. I need to know what's going on up there. Whoever is putting armed guards on a hiking path has to be up to no good. They shouldn't be up there. If what they were doing was even close to being legitimate, then they wouldn't need some jerk standing around with a rifle keeping people out."

Andrea nodded at Seth, but turned to look at Mel. "He's right, something is wrong up there. I can't help myself either, I want to know just what."

Mel sighed. "Okay, I'm in. When do we go?"

Seth looked out the cabin window that faced the lake. "We'll wait a couple more hours. It's not dark enough yet." Seth laughed. "That reminds me, I better throw in some flashlights too."

As she studied Seth's determined face. Andrea frowned. "How come I get the feeling you already think we can get to that hill? I mean, if they have a guard on that trail now, I'm sure there's more like him up on the hill."

Seth's brown eyes sparkled. "Oh, I'm pretty sure I can get us in. I've already told you my family has been in all the areas around Hidden Lake. My brothers and I covered a lot of area when we were young and in that time, we've been able to expose a lot of her secrets."

Shaking her head. Mel frowned. "That might be, but do you also have a plan for getting away from that place after we take a look?"

Now both Andrea and Melanie stared at Seth. Neither liked the moment of hesitation before Seth finally smiled and answered Mel's question.

"Don't worry, we'll find a way. Like I said, the two of you don't have to come with me. I'd understand if you wanted to stay here. Hell, if I wasn't so curious myself, I'd be drinking a beer and doing some fishing instead of heading out in the woods in the dark."

The two women exchanged glances and then Andrea smiled. "Count us in."

Seth's face lit up and he rubbed his hands together. "Great, now I think we should grab some food. By the time we eat, it should be time to head out."

Andrea laughed. "Why did I know that was coming? Okay Mel, let's scrounge this guy up some food."

Chapter 4

The trio finished eating and then sat around the cabin until an hour after the sun had faded behind the mountains. Seth decided then it was dark enough and figured it was time for the three of them to put on their packs and head out of the cabin.

When they stepped outside and Seth headed in the opposite direction than the one he had taken earlier, Andrea frowned. "I'll be the first to admit that I'm not the greatest with directions, but aren't we going the wrong way Seth?"

Turning back from his lead position to look at Andrea and Mel behind him, Seth smiled. "I know where there's a trail that will take us to the far side of that hill. There's a cave over that way too. I don't think anyone but my brothers and I know about it. If we can head inside of that cave, it will take us to just about where we saw that damn guard. It is a little further to go this way, but I also think it will be a hell of a lot safer."

Andrea nodded. "Safer sounds good to me."

Pointing at the two women, Seth's face was serious. "I want both of you to stay close behind me. If you can't keep up, just give me a holler and let me know. It's damn easy to get lost out here."

Melanie shook her head. "You don't have to worry about that. We'll keep up. You're the only one that knows the area."

Seth waited for Andrea to nod her own agreement before he turned and began walking, both women closed behind. Seth was the only one who held a flashlight, but it wasn't turned on. Right now, the moon was bright enough, they could see enough to walk. Although even with the moons' light shining down to guide them, both Andrea and Mel still tripped more than once over the branches, rocks and numerous pine cones lying in the grass covered path. The further they went, the trail looked less and less like it had ever even seen human traffic. In fact it didn't look like many animals had used it recently either.

When Seth stopped suddenly in front of her, Andrea bumped into him and mumbled an apology. "Sorry, I didn't realize you were stopping."

Seth put a finger to his lips and spoke in a whisper. "That's okay, but we're getting close. We're going to have to keep our talking to a minimum and stay as quiet as possible."

Instead of answering, both women only nodded their understanding. Just ahead of them they could see the dark outline of a large hill. Seth pointed at a clump of bushes at the base and again spoke quietly. "Behind those bushes is where we go in.

You'll have to crawl at first, but then the tunnel opens up into a cave and we'll be able to stand. Just keep your eyes open, I have no idea what to expect in there. Remember you have your bear spray in your packs and your pocket knives if you need them."

Andrea sighed. "Yeah, but let's hope we don't have to use them."

Stepping over to the bushes, Seth pushed them aside. He also had to take the time to move away some rocks and dirt that had fallen in front of the entrance before the three could see the narrow entryway. Seth turned on his flashlight and pointed the beam down toward the ground in front of the tunnel, before clicking it off and turning to face Andrea and Mel.
"We'll going to need this after we get inside. Are you both doing okay?"

Andrea nodded and Mel shrugged before answering in a hushed voice. "As okay as I can be. There aren't any spiders or animals in that place are there?"

Seth shook his head, but Mel saw the slight grin that had snuck across his face. "Don't worry, they're more scared of you than you are of them."

Mel rolled her eyes. "I doubt that. Let's just go in before I chicken out."

Seth crawled in first, followed by Mel and then Andrea. Luckily, with the flashlight turned back on, but that Seth held pointed ahead of them, neither woman could see what might be slithering or crawling on the cave walls as they entered.

They didn't have to crawl very far before, as Seth had told them it would, the entrance opened up into the larger cave.
Seth's voice was quiet as he spoke.
"We're standing on the far side of the hill from where we were earlier. There's a series of small caves and tunnels in here. Just stick

close to me, I've been here before and know the way."

As the three began to walk, Seth kept his flashlight focused downward and shielded the lens with one hand, afraid if someone was in the caves they would see even the meager light it gave off. As they continued further into the caves, Seth realized the tunnels seemed to have more light than he remembered from the hundreds of times he and his brothers had explored through them. As he stared ahead of him, it dawned on Seth why the light was better.

He turned back to look at the two women behind him and then pointing ahead, he whispered.

"I think this is about to get interesting."

Both Andrea and Mel were so focused on following Seth's lead that neither had noticed that the interior of the cave and the area ahead of them was brighter than where they had first entered, until Seth pointed it out. Andrea groaned when she realized what was happening. "Oh hell, they really are in here."

Melanie nodded. "And whoever they are, you can bet they don't want company."

Seth looked around the space. "There's another tunnel to the right, it should bypass the area where that light is coming from. If I remember right, it turns back and we might be able to find a few places where we can see into the larger cave without being noticed. No more talking though, just stay close."

Neither Andrea nor Mel needed to be reminded of that. Both were too anxious to carry a conversation as they followed Seth through the semi-dark insides of the hill.

Andrea was behind Seth with Mel so close behind her that once in a while she could feel her friend's body bump into her arm. For Andrea the touch was reassuring and she was glad for not only Mel's closeness, but also for the fact that Seth was only a step ahead of her. Of course, if it wasn't for Seth, she knew she would have never had found the courage to even be here. Despite her enormous curiosity about what might be happening up here.

Seth stopped again and turned off the flashlight that was still pointed toward the tunnel floor. Even though the light around them had been enough to be able to see to walk, the difference now seemed to plunge them into darkness.

As their eyes adjusted, the women could see Seth was reaching up and feeling along the tunnel wall.

Stepping back and leaning over Andrea, he whispered in her ear. "There's a shelf like ledge just above the top of my head. I'm going to boost you up first and then Melanie. I want the two of you to slide along the ledge, but be careful, the rock is crumbling. Just on the other side of this wall is where that light is coming from. Don't expose yourself. We don't want to take a chance of being seen."

Taking a deep breath to try and calm her nerves, Andrea nodded. Seth took the time to reach over and touch Mel's shoulder and then he pointed up before pointing over at Andrea. He waited for Mel's nod that she understood and then turned back to Andrea. Clasping his hands together, he lowered them in front of her. Andrea put her foot in Seth's hands, shaped like a horse stirrup, and he lifted her up. Andrea slid her hands along the wall to keep her balance. As she did, Andrea could feel the rocks and dirt scrape into the sensitive skin on her palms. As Seth lifted her higher, Andrea felt for the ledge. As soon as she found the indent where the ledge began, she placed both hands on it and let Seth push her until she was able to crawl up on the nature made shelf.

Seth repeated the same process with Mel and then he jumped and grabbed a hold of a jutted out rock and pulled himself up to join his friends. The three rested a moment before Andrea crawled along the narrow ledge and toward a spot where she could see a beam of light shining through. Mel and Seth crawled behind her.

At the break in the wall, Andrea leaned forward just far enough to peek around the edge. It wasn't just the men standing in the room that made her gasp and pull back quickly. It was more the object in the cave the men were guarding that was the cause of her excitement. Just as Andrea was about to yell out, Seth reached over and covered her mouth with his hand, shaking his head. Above the hand, Andrea's eyes widened and darted back and forth anxiously. It took her a moment to realize what Seth was doing and why. As she did, Andrea relaxed and nodded her head slightly. Pulling away his hand, Seth motioned for them to switch places. The two carefully moved around each other on the narrow ledge.

Taking Andrea's place, Seth peered into the cave. Seeing armed guards, Seth's brown eyes narrowed. Then, looking at the object that had caused Andrea's excitement, Seth frowned. He wasn't convinced the item was actually what it appeared to be and knew he definitely wanted a closer look. Backing away from the entrance, he motioned for Mel to come over and take her own look.

Slowly the three maneuvered around until Mel was at the opening. As she stared in astonishment at the room's contents, one of the guards turned from looking at the object he guarded and glanced over her way. Pulling back quickly, Mel's leg kicked out, knocking some rocks loose. As they tumbled to the ground, the clattering noise seemed extremely loud in the otherwise quiet area. Mel cursed under her breath.

The sound of one of the guard's hollering to the other could be heard.

"Hey, someone's on the other side of that wall. Quick, get over there. We can't let whoever's on the other side out of the cave."

Hearing the guards' words, Seth jumped off the ledge and then helped first Andrea and then Melanie down. Grabbing Andrea's hand, Seth tugged on her arm. Not bothering to lower his voice now, Seth yelled. "Grab a hold of Mel's hand and hold on tight. We have to get the hell out of here and I don't want to leave either of you behind."

Grabbing Mel's hand, Andrea turned to her friend. "Hang on, Seth's going to lead us out and fast."

The three began running, Seth in the lead and both women close behind. All of them ran for their lives back through the tunnels they had just come into. Andrea and Mel being pulled along as they tripped and stumbled blindly until they found themselves at the tunnel entrance. Letting go of Andrea's hand, Seth let her and Mel crawl out first. A moment later, the trio was standing outside and once again joined hands as they took off running.

Andrea felt like her arm was going to be pulled clean out of the socket as the larger and faster Seth hauled her behind him. As they ran, the moon, now standing high up in the night sky, provided some light. Even with that, all three were still having a hard time navigating the trail.

Andrea tripped over a branch and stumbled. When she felt Mel's hand slip from hers, she knew her friend must have found the same obstacle. The blood curdling scream that followed stopped both Andrea and Seth dead in their tracks. Seeing Mel on the ground, Seth turned back and knelt down beside her. "Are you okay?"

Grabbing her leg, Mel let out a high pitched scream that came through clenched teeth.

Taking that for an answer, Seth reached down and slipping his arms under Mel's body, he lifted his friend off the ground, cradling her in his arms.

"I'm sorry to hurt you even more than you already are Mel, but we need to get the hell out of here. I'm sure those guards can't be too far behind us."

He turned to Andrea. "Just stay with me."

Nodding at Seth, but staring at the pain evident on Mel's face, Andrea ran behind Seth. Even though he was carrying the extra burden of Mel's weight, Seth almost matched the pace he had been on before the untimely accident.

Out of breath, Andrea sighed with relief as the cabin finally came into view.

Carrying Mel in, Seth laid her on the couch, his brown eyes full of compassion as he stared at Mel's pain filled expression. "I'm sorry, but I need to take a look at that leg. I'll try to be careful."

Closing her eyes, Mel let out a moan. Seth frowned, concerned. "Keep your eyes open. I don't want you passing out on me. You might have injured your head when you hit the ground. I need you to stay awake until we're sure."

Mel's eyes opened, she did feel like the room was spinning. That scared her and she opened her eyes even wider. As soon as Seth saw her looking at him, he gave her a reassuring smile and then moved so he could look at her leg. It only took one glance for Seth to know they'd have to make a flying trip to the hospital in Hagen Falls. Although the bone hadn't broken through the skin on Mel's lower leg, he could see it pushing out against her skin and knew it wouldn't be long until the bone actually cut through. Moving away from the leg, Seth reached up and placed a hand on Mel's sweat soaked forehead. "Don't worry, we're going to get you to town and get you fixed up. We'll have to take your car, where's your keys?"

Mel took a shaky breath, trying not to scream. The pain in her leg was excruciating and the back of her head, against the couch was beginning to throb. She was certain now she had slammed her head into the ground when she had fallen. At the time, the pain in her leg had overridden any other wounds she might have suffered. Now though, both pains were steady. Melanie gritted her teeth. "My purse…in…bedroom."

Standing behind Seth, Andrea nodded. "Don't worry, I'll grab your purse." She was glad to get out of the room for a moment. The sight of her friend in so much pain was hard to watch. Heading into the bedroom, Andrea grabbed not only Mel's purse, but her own. She glanced over at their bags, but knew she would be coming back for those. Seth would need to come back up here to get his truck once they got Mel fixed up. Andrea ran back into the living room. Seth was still kneeling on the floor next to Melanie.

He turned to Andrea. "Go out and unlock the car, then I'm going to need your help. I can carry Mel out, but you'll have to open doors for me."

Finally between the two of them, Seth and Andrea were able to get Mel half way comfortable in the back seat of Mels' car. The two got in front, with Seth behind the wheel. Starting the car, he turned to face Andrea. "I need you to talk to Mel and keep her awake. I'm afraid of a concussion, I saw a lot of those when I was playing football. They can cause a lot of damage. I'll drive as carefully as I can."

Andrea nodded and then knelt in the seat, so she was facing backwards where she could keep an eye on her friend.

Reaching over the top of the seat, she grabbed Mel's hand and held it tight. Then she started talking, making sure her friend joined her in the conversation.

Half listening to them, Seth pulled away from the cabin and began the drive toward town.

Chapter 5

The drive from the cabin to town seemed to take an eternity to the occupants of the car. Finally though, Seth pulled Mels' car into the emergency entrance of the small hospital in Hagen Falls. As he opened the car door, he turned to Andrea. "Wait here, I'll get some help."

Not waiting for a response, Seth jumped out of the car and rushed through the double glass doors that took him inside Hagen Falls only hospital. After he'd gone, Andrea tried to give a reassuring smile to Mel. "We're at the hospital Mel. We'll have you fixed up in no time at all."

As she tried to respond, Mel instead moaned in pain and Andrea felt her heart clench. Was there anything worse than seeing someone you loved in pain?

Luckily, Andrea didn't have time to ponder the question that had popped into her head as she saw two men pushing a gurney, followed close behind by Seth.

From there, everything was a blur to Andrea as Mel was rushed inside. Her best friend in the world was being wheeled away on the gurney with Doctors and nurses shouting instructions, Andrea didn't understand.

As Mel was pushed down the hall, Andrea was now sure she heard either a Doctor or a nurse hollering something about prepping for surgery. Before she realized it was even happening, Mel was pushed out of her sight and Andrea found herself ushered into a waiting room, by one of the nurses, and where she found herself sitting beside Seth. The two were the only people in the room. Seth reached over and covered the hands Andrea had been wringing together nervously with his own. "She's going to be okay Andrea. I'm sure her leg is broken, but they will know how to take care of that here."

Nodding, Andrea looked at Seth, despite his words, she could see the same worry she was feeling echoed on his face. "Oh my gosh Seth, I need to call her family. I know they'd want to be here."

Although Andrea knew that Mel's cell phone with all her contact numbers was in the purse belonging to her friend and that she had carried in with her own, she instead grabbed her own cell phone and used it to make the call she wished she didn't have to.

Dialing the number she knew by heart, even though Mel hadn't live at her parents' home for years, she waited anxiously for someone to pick up the phone. Andrea didn't realize how late it was until she heard Maria Grayden's groggy "Hello".

It was bad enough for Andrea to know she had apparently got hold of a sleeping lady, but she had bad news to share as well.

Andrea drew a deep breath. "Maria, this is Andrea. I'm sorry to have to wake you up. I'm afraid I have bad news, Melanie has had an accident. I'm sure her leg is broken. Seth and I are here at the emergency room. Mel is still in with the Doctors. We haven't been told anything yet, but I knew you'd want to be here."

Fully awake now, Maria was still speechless a moment as she took in what Andrea was saying. A call in the middle of the night always seemed to carry bad news with it. Maria's voice finally came back on the line. "We'll be right down. I'll call Paul, I know he'll want to be with his sister. Olivia is already here with us, on vacation from school. We'll bring her also. The more people we can gather to pray for Melanie the better. Don't worry, we'll be there as soon as we can."

As Andrea hung up, she had to smile. With Marias' great faith on Mels' side, Andrea already felt better about her friends' chances of a quick recovery. Putting her phone away, Andrea turned to Seth. "They'll be here. I just wish that Doctor would come in and give us some information. I hate not knowing what's happening."

Seth stood up and held out his hand. "C'mon let's go find a coffee machine. I think we could both use it."

Nodding, Andrea grabbed Seth's hand and let him pull her up. The two left the waiting room and headed down to the reception desk where they were given no information on Mel, but were given directions to a room full of vending machines.

Standing in front of the coffee machine, Andrea turned to see Seth at another machine where he was grabbing a package of miniature doughnuts. When he pointed at the machine and asked Andrea if she wanted some, the head of light brown hair shook back and forth, as she placed an arm across her waist. "No thanks, I think my stomach is too upset to even try to eat anything right now."

Seth laughed. "That's strange, food always seems to settle my stomach down."

Andrea smiled. "I could have guessed that." She shook her head wearily. "C'mon, let's head back to the waiting room. I don't want to miss the Doctor if he comes back."

Ten minutes after they returned to the room and were sitting mostly in worried silence, Mel's family came in.

After exchanged hugs, everyone sat down and Seth tried to explain about the accident, with Mel tripping and getting hurt.
"We shouldn't have been out hiking in the dark. Mel must have just tripped over a rock or something. We got her down here as fast as we could." Apologizing as he told the story, Seth also left out any mention of the

guards who had been at the hill or the real story as to why the three friends had been at the caves by Hidden Lake.

Mels' dad shook his head as he listened to Seth's apology. "I'm just glad you were there to carry her out."

Maria nodded. "Daniel's right, without you, Melanie might still be lying up in that place."

Seth shook his head. "It was my idea for the three of us to go camping up there in the first place. I take complete responsibility."

Maria took Seth's hand. "It's not your fault. Now we all just have to pray she is going to be okay."

Maria asked everyone to join hands and then they bowed their heads as Maria gave a heartfelt prayer for Melanie's quick recovery.

Right after Maria finished, a man in a white Doctors' coat stepped into the room. He looked over to where Maria and Daniel were now sitting with Seth and Andrea.

"Are you Mister and Missus Grayden?" As soon as the couple nodded, the Doctor continued. "Your daughter is stable and resting. She had a compound fracture of her tibia. We've completed the surgery and it went well. Melanie will have to wear a cast for at least twelve weeks and a she'll have a lot of rehabilitation when the cast is removed, but I think the bone will heal well and she shouldn't have any complications."

Everyone in the room seemed to sigh with relief at the same time. Maria stood and took the Doctors' hand. "Thank you so much, when can we see her?"

The Doctor pointed at the door. "You can go in now, but only for a few minutes. Melanie needs to rest. Although we discovered she also bumped her head in the fall, we saw no signs of concussion, so she was given a painkiller. She is going to be groggy and a bit disoriented. I would also like to keep her here at least a day or two for observation."

As the Doctor turned toward the door, the small group followed him out of the waiting room and down the hall to the room where Mel lay on the hospital bed. She had an IV drip running in her arm and a large cast on her leg. She looked tiny and pale, her eyes closed.

Maria was the first to step over to the bed. Her husband stepped up next to her. Both parents stared down at their daughter with anguish and love clearly evident on their faces. Maria carefully brushed back Mel's hair and the young woman's eyes opened. The eyelids fluttered like they were too heavy for Mel to hold open.

Maria bent down and kissed her daughter's forehead. "Everything's okay now honey. We're all here and you're going to be okay, thank the Lord for his miracles."

Daniel, sliding one arm around his wife's waist took hold of his daughter's hand with his free hand. "We're just glad Seth and Andrea got you to the hospital as quickly as they did."

Mel sighed her eyes drooping. "Mom, Dad, thanks for coming. I'm sorry, I'm just so tired."

Maria nodded. "Of course you are. You've been through a lot and the Doctor said they gave you pain medication that will help you sleep. The awful accident is all over now though and you need to get some rest. Your father and I will be staying and sitting right here if you need us. Olivia is here with us and Paul is on his way."

Olivia, who could almost be a twin to her sister, stepped closer so Mel could see her. "That's right Mel, I'm here as long as you need me and I can't wait to put my autograph on that cast of yours."

Mel smiled wearily. She felt like she was floating on a lake with the warm sun soaking into her bones and making her tired. It was a relaxing feeling and she began drifting off to sleep, the voices around her receding.
Just before she succumbed totally, she heard Andrea saying she and Seth would be back in the morning.

Unsure if Mel had heard her, Andrea turned to Maria and handed her Mel's purse.
"This is Mel's, her cellphone is in there if she needs it. Seth and I had to use Mel's car to get her here. We'll go ahead and take it over to her place. I don't think she'll be driving for a while though. I'll bring her keys back with me in the morning when we come to visit."

Looking at her watch, Maria smiled. "It actually is morning. You and Seth need to get some rest too. All of you have been through quite an ordeal. If Melanie wakes up before you return, I'll let her know what's going on."

Maria hugged Andrea and then Seth before she smiled at them with tears in her eyes. "Thanks for getting my baby to the hospital where she could get fixed up. Daniel and I will watch over her now. You and Seth go home. We'll see you both later."

Hating to leave, but knowing it was the best thing to do right now, Andrea and Seth walked out of the room.

Going back through the hospital, the two made their way outside to Mel's car. Andrea looked at Seth. "Why don't you drive me over to my house? I can get my car and follow you to Mel's place and then I can drive you home."

As he pulled away from the hospital, Seth shook his head. "I'm so sorry about this mess I got the two of you in."

Andrea frowned. "Hey, don't you dare blame yourself. You didn't twist our arms and force us up to that place. We were just as curious as you, probably more so."

Even though he still felt guilty, Seth had to smile at Andrea's words. The two had made it to Andrea's place. She got in her car and then followed Seth as he drove Mel's car to her house. Parking the car, Seth locked it up and then walked over to where Andrea waited. As he jumped in the car, he handed Andrea Mel's keys. Then settled in the seat for the short drive to his own house.

Pulling in his driveway, Andrea turned off the car, but neither got out. Instead, Andrea turned to Seth, her face filled with anxiety. "Do you think that thing we saw up in the cave was real? I mean a real ship that came from outer space?"

Seth shrugged. "I don't know. I wish we could have gotten a better look. If it is real, why would anyone hide such an amazing discovery? If it's a man-made vehicle, why are they hiding that kind of technology from the world? Did you happen to look at the ceiling in that cave?"

Andrea shook her head. "All I noticed was the spaceship, oh, and the armed guards that were in the cave. I was so worried about getting caught, I didn't spend more time looking. I can't believe we were able to get away. I didn't even think about it when we had the emergency of getting Mel out of there, but we were damn lucky those guards didn't chase us down." Andrea frowned, thinking of Seth's question. "Why, what did you see on the ceiling?"

Seth's forehead wrinkled, his dark eyes worried. "I'm almost certain that cave had a regular ceiling, instead of one made of rock. I didn't get a real close look, but it also looked like the type of roof that could be opened, like the whole thing was on a hinge or something. I thought I saw two pieces of ceiling with a split down the middle."

Andrea frowned. "Oh wow, you don't think that ship actually flies do you?"

Nodding, Seth let out a sigh. "I do and I think it might be what people thought was an actual UFO sighting. It also might explain those strange lights people saw in the sky over the years."

Silent a moment thinking, Andrea stared at Seth. "Maybe it really is a UFO and from another world, not a ship that was man made here on earth."

Seth shrugged. "It might be, but I think something else is going on up there. Whatever it is, someone doesn't want anyone else knowing about it. Those guards looked to me either to be military or some kind of mercenaries the government hired and there's no way in hell they should even be up at a public recreation area. When I go up to get my truck tomorrow, or rather later today, I want to do some more looking around. I don't expect you to go with me, other than maybe to give me a ride to the cabin. With what happened to Mel, you probably don't even want to go near that place again. I can't say as I'd blame you if you felt that way."

Staring at Seth, Andrea smiled, her blue eyes sparkling. "You're wrong about that Seth. I want to know what they are really hiding. The fact that they are concealing something not only makes me really mad, but a lot more curious. I just need a nap and a shower first. As soon as I get that, I'll be back to pick you up. We can stop by the hospital and visit Mel before we head back up to Hidden Lake."

Seth couldn't believe what he was hearing. "Are you sure? I'd love to have you with me, but I'd understand if you wanted to just stay here in town."

Andrea started the car. "Just get some rest and I'll be back in a few hours."

Seth smiled. "It's a deal. I'll see you later then."

Andrea waited until Seth walked to his house and unlocked the door before she backed out of the driveway and headed home for the nap and shower she had told Seth she needed.

Walking in his house, the first thing Seth did was head for the fridge and make himself a sandwich. Carrying his food into the living room, he turned on the TV set and then muted the sound. Seth needed the light the TV made to chase away shadows, but didn't want the distraction of the noise. He needed time to think. It was funny, but his mind kept going back to when Andrea had asked him about the gold necklace he had found. Seth had always wondered about that necklace and who it had originally belonged to. When he had first found it, his parents had even placed an ad in the towns' weekly paper under the lost and found section. They hadn't even gotten one call from anyone claiming the small treasure. Thinking of the necklace, Seth stood up from the couch and went to his bedroom. In his closet, he pulled down a box where he kept not only the necklace, but other strange things he had found over the years. There always seemed to be something new and interesting to be found around Hidden Lake. All you had to do was keep an eye out.

Pulling the necklace from the box, Seth carried it into the living room. Once he sat down, Seth picked his laptop up off the coffee table in front of him and opened it. The he began searching.

Somehow, he just knew the necklace was a clue to the strange happenings at Hidden Lake. Years ago when Seth asked a friend who knew antiques and jewelry to look at the necklace, he had figured the piece had been made some time in the thirties or forties but was surprised at its' value. Searching various websites now, he found a piece of jewelry similar to the one he still held in his hand. Seth stared amazed at how much the value that had been placed on the piece had risen. It was a lot more than the price he had been quoted years ago.

It was another link on the page that caught his attention though. Frowning at the name of the link, he clicked on it. Seth was taken to a website he'd never heard of before, but one that included a documentary video.

As Seth watched, everything began to make disturbing sense to him. When the video finally ended, Seth hoped he was wrong in his conclusions as to what was happening up at Hidden Lake. He wished now that what was going on up there actually was a UFO, manmade or otherwise, and not something related to the documentary the link had taken him to. Seth saved his searches, knowing he would be sharing them with Andrea.

Standing up, he stretched and yawned. Looking back down at his seat on the couch,

Seth decided it looked comfortable enough and decided to just take a quick nap there, rather than head to his bed. Seth sat back down and then stretched his body out on the couch, his head touching the arm rest on one side and his feet just about hanging off the one on the other end.

He didn't plan on really being able to fall asleep, when a knock on the door had him sitting up quickly and made him realize he had actually been sound asleep.
Seth was disoriented a moment, then the events from earlier came flooding back.

Standing, Seth rushed to the front door where Andrea stood holding two cups of coffee and a copy of the local newspaper. The Hagen Falls Sunday Paper was also the only paper the small town had all week.

Andrea held one of the cups out toward Seth. "I thought you could use this."

Taking the Styrofoam cup, Seth nodded. "Just what I needed. I didn't even get a pot ready to brew. In fact, I was still sleeping when I heard your knock."

Andrea looked at her watch and nodded. "It's actually closer to lunch than breakfast and I'm still tired."

Seth opened the door wider. "Come on in, I need to change before we head over to see Mel. I fell asleep on the couch in my clothes from yesterday."

Andrea held up the newspaper she was holding. "You may want to take a look at this first."

Seth frowned, but led Andrea to the living room and over to the couch before he pointed at the paper. "What's going on?"

Andrea handed the paper to Seth and let him read the front page headlines for himself. Which he did, out loud and in shock. "Hidden Lake Recreation Area closed to public. Warnings of toxic spill have residents concerned."

Seth frowned. "What the hell is that all about?"

Andrea shrugged. "I think it would be better if you just read the article for yourself."

Seth stared at her a moment before turning his attention to the story that had made headlines on the small town paper's front page. It only took him a moment to read what he knew were obvious lies. "This says two semi-trucks carrying toxic waste wrecked up by Hidden Lake yesterday. We know there was no wreck."

Andrea nodded. "Apparently we must have gotten a little too close to whatever they were hiding up there. Now they're closing the whole place up, trying to keep others away. It says they have roadblocks set up, even to the road that leads to your cabin."

Seth shook his head. "That's probably just the main roads. Don't worry, I know more than one way into that cabin."

Seth opened his laptop. "I found something interesting I want you to look at too." Pointing at the necklace on the table, Seth turned to Andrea. "That's the necklace I told you and Mel about." Bringing up the site that showed the value of his necklace, Seth pointed at the picture with the estimated value.

Andrea's eyes widened. "Is that right? Seth, c'mon, that says your necklace is worth ten thousand dollars."

Seth nodded. "I think it's probably worth even more than that. I'm going to have you watch this documentary and then maybe you can understand why. I'm going to hurry and get dressed while you're looking at it. Then we can decide the best way to handle this whole situation."

Andrea nodded and Seth handed her the laptop. He clicked the play button before leaving to go and change.

By the time Seth returned, the video had finished and Andrea had leaned forward to pick up the necklace Seth had left on the table.

She stared at it mesmerized. Her fingers touched the symbol at the end of the gold chain. Using one finger she gently traced the symbol over and over again. She knew it was the Star of David. The symbol was encrusted with jewels. The website had claimed they were diamonds and the necklace an antiquity because of where it had come from. The vintage look of the necklace left no doubt in Andrea's mind that the jewels that made a luster on the symbol were in fact actual diamonds. The necklace was fairly heavy and she remembered Seth saying it was twenty four karat gold.

When Seth returned, he took a seat next to

Andrea and she jumped. So lost in studying the necklace after watching the video, she'd forgotten Seth was only in the other room changing clothes. The hand not holding the necklace went to her chest. "Oh hell Seth, you about scared me to death."

Seth laughed. "Sorry about that."

Andrea frowned. "That doesn't sound like a very sincere apology."

Before Seth could reply, Andrea shook her head. "Never mind, it was my fault."
She pointed at the laptop. "Do you really believe this documentary explains what's happening up at Hidden Lake?"

Seth nodded. ""That or something a hell of a lot like it. The people that made that documentary didn't specify Hidden Lake, but it sounds like the same type of place they've found other things just like this hidden."
Seth pointed at the necklace Andrea still held. "That could be the proof that the same

thing is going on up at Hidden Lake and why they are trying to keep people out."

Seth took a gulp of his coffee. "I think we need to go visit Mel and then find a way to get to my cabin. Once we get there, we can try and figure out our next step."

Chapter 6

Seth and Andrea headed for the hospital, where they found Mel sitting up in her hospital bed and looking a hundred percent better than she had a few short hours ago. Andrea stepped over and gave Mel a big hug. Then stepping back, she handed her friend her keys. "We took your car to your house." Andrea stared at Mel and smiled. "Mel it's so good to see you sitting up. How are you feeling?"

Mel smiled. "It would seem a lot better than I could have been, thanks to both of you. I can't remember a lot after I got here, but I can remember before that and I can't tell you how much I appreciate the two of you bringing me here. You saved my life."

Seth shook his head. "I wouldn't say that, and there's no need to thank us." Looking around the room, Seth frowned. "I thought your family would be here."

Mel nodded. "They just left a few minutes ago to grab some coffee and breakfast down in the cafeteria. Poor mom and dad, they stayed up watching me. I know they must be drained. I tried to get them to go home, but they wouldn't hear of it."
Mel turned to Andrea. "Thanks a lot for calling them."

Andrea laughed. "You weren't in any shape to make that call. I was glad to do it."

Mel looked at her two friends. "What are you two going to do now? Are you going back up to the cabin?"

Seth shrugged. "We might have to go get my truck, but there's no hurry."

Mel nodded. "I would love to head back up there with you two." Mel pointed at her cast.

"I think my hiking days are a ways in the future though."

Seth smiled. "You just get better, there will be plenty of time for hiking after your leg gets better. Is it hurting you?"

Mel shrugged and shook her head. "I think they're keeping my pain meds pretty steady for today at least. Hopefully I won't be in here long and then I will be headed for mom and dad's place. They want me to stay there until I get a walking cast to replace this one. Right now, I'm going to be sitting in a wheelchair. I'm just thankful they're willing to help me. I've never had any kind of broken bone before."

Andrea laughed. "Hey, at least you won't have to go back to the factory for a while. So this dark cloud has a silver lining anyway."

Melanie smiled. "I guess there is that."

The two friends stayed and visited with Mel for a little while and then looked at each other, both of them knowing they should be getting up to the cabin. Luckily for them, Mel yawned and gave them an excuse to get moving.

Telling Mel to take it easy and promising to visit soon, they left the hospital.

Neither Seth nor Andrea thought it would take long to explore the cave at Hidden Lake again and knew they would be visiting with Melanie at her parents' home soon enough. Neither had shared with her what they had discovered on Seth's laptop, figuring it was better and a whole lot safer to wait and tell her about the documentary after they found out the truth behind what was happening at Hidden Lake. That way, if they did happen to get caught, no one could connect Mel to what they were doing. By the time they finished their investigation, hopefully, Mel would be out of the hospital and recuperating at her parents' house.

Because Seth knew the area, he was driving Andrea's car. Turning off the main road, he took a side road, that to Andrea, didn't look like much more than the hiking trail they'd all been hiking on when Mel had injured her leg.

Taking her eyes from the barely discernable road, Andrea stared over at Seth. "Is my car going to make it through here?"

Seth smiled, but kept his eyes on the road. "Don't worry, I've driven cars a lot lower than yours up here. We'll make it to the cabin. From there, we'll have to either use my truck, or more than likely, you should prepare yourself for some hiking."

Andrea nodded, but didn't speak as she focused her attention on the path Seth was navigating. It was a half an hour of rough road and careful driving, before Andrea saw the cabin ahead of them, and let out a relieved sigh.

Hearing the sound, Seth laughed. "Hey, wait a minute, does that sound mean you didn't trust me to get us up here?"

Andrea shook her head. "Oh, I trust you Seth, I just don't trust my car. The poor thing is used to city driving."

Seth smiled. "Hey, sometimes that's a lot worse than that old road we just came through."

Seth pulled the car in next to his truck and parked. "I think we should head inside and see if we can put ourselves together a couple of backpacks and maybe grab some lunch. I'm starving, I didn't have anything but coffee for breakfast."

Andrea covered her mouth with her hands in feigned shock as she looked at Seth. "Oh my hell, you poor thing, you may waste away to nothing. I better hurry and dig you up some food."

Opening his door, Seth shook his head. "Very funny Andrea. I happen to be twice your size and I also should warn you, I get ornery when not fed regularly."

Shaking her head, Andrea pushed open her own car door. "Well, we can't have that, lunch will be my number one priority."

Seth laughed as he walked to the cabin and opened the door to let Andrea step in. True to her word, as soon as she got inside, Andrea rushed to the kitchen where she hastily began heating up leftover spaghetti. She added a couple of grilled cheese sandwiches to complete their meal and satisfy Seth's appetite.

As soon as they finished eating, Andrea washed up the few dishes they had used, while Seth got busy filling their backpacks. This time he added in ropes, rock picks, protein bars and a first aid kit to the things that they had packed before. Pulling out his cell phone from his pocket, Seth also threw it in one of the bags. "I can't get a signal on that damn thing up here, but you never know what might come in handy."

Andrea handed her purse to Seth and he put it in the other pack. Andrea sighed watching him. "I really wish Mel was up here with us. I know she'd love uncovering a conspiracy. She's fascinating by things like that. She's always watching those types of shows on TV."

Seth shrugged. "I just hope we can figure out what is really happening. When we do, we can share all of it with her."

Smiling, Andrea nodded. "It might be easier with just the two of us anyway."

Seth handed Andrea her backpack. "Slip that on and see if it feels okay. I don't think it will be too heavy for you to carry."

Taking the pack from Seth and slipping it on, Andrea adjusted the straps, bounced the pack a couple of times, and then gave a nod. "It feels fine."

Seth nodded back. "Great, because I think we will be better off if we stick to just hiking up there. I've decided I don't want to take a chance on anyone hearing the sound of my truck. I'd rather they didn't have any idea we're coming their way."

Eyes wide, Andrea nodded. "My feelings exactly."

With Seth leading the way, the two left the cabin and headed along a tree lined trail toward the hill where they'd seen the vehicle that looked like a space ship and hopefully to some answers.

As they got close, Seth once again found a tunnel for them to crawl in.
Andrea was pretty sure it wasn't the same one they'd been in the night before.
Although she was just as certain most caves in the area looked a lot alike.

This time, entering the tunnel, after being out in the midday sunlight, both Andrea and Seth had to stop and wait a few minutes for their eyes to adjust to the almost lightless tunnel.

Seth took Andrea's hand. "No matter what happens, don't you dare let go."

Andrea shook her head. "Don't worry, that's the last thing on my mind. I'm hanging on for dear life, believe me."

The two began walking slowly, listening for any unfamiliar sounds. They didn't have to walk very far before they could hear the voices of two men coming to them from a place nearby.

"Hey, did you hear about Beckman?"

"Yeah, and I heard he won't be pulling duty up here anymore. Wherever they put him, you can bet it's not guarding this damn phony spaceship."

The sound of both men laughing floated to Andrea and Seth, who were staring dumbfounded at each other. Even though Seth had said he thought the ship was manmade, it was still disappointing to hear the truth. For Andrea, who still held out hope for alien visitors from another world, hearing the men speak the words was heartbreaking.

Seth felt his hopes drop too, but thought that at least now they knew at least some of the truth. They also had a lot more to uncover and no idea yet how to go about doing that. Seth pulled on Andrea's arm, drawing her back the way they had come in.

Andrea frowned, but followed easily behind the man. At least they seemed to have figured out the spaceship was a lie. That made Andrea wonder in astonishment if the rest of Seth's theory might really be close to the truth also. If he was right, that was something the government or the military would definitely want to keep a closely guarded secret.

Andrea's thoughts were interrupted as Seth stopped walking and she realized they had made it back to the tunnel entrance. She waited until they both had crawled out before turning to Seth, her face wrinkled in curiosity. "What are we doing? Why did we leave? I thought you wanted to take a better look in that cave?"

Seth shook his head. "That place is just a decoy. They must use that spaceship to keep people's attention away from what is really happening. I think they must flash lights out through the top of that cave once in a while, maybe even fly that ship out. We have to consider the possibility that whatever they're hiding is somewhere else. Remember, there are caves in all the hills around Hidden Lake."

Andrea shook her head. "If they're all over, then how do you plan on finding the right cave whatever they are really hiding is in?"

Seth smiled, his brown eyes dancing. "We're going on a stakeout."

The blue eyes staring at him widened. "What the hell does that mean? I'm no detective Seth, I don't know the first thing about any kind of stakeout."

Shrugging, Seth shook his head. "Neither do I, not really, but I am a huge fan of old cop shows." Seth smiled. "How hard can it be? We're going to go around to the other side of the lake where we'll have a good vantage point. Sooner or later someone is going to head to that other cave where the real secrets lie. We just have to wait and watch where they head. Then when it gets darker we just head over to that cave ourselves. We have cameras on our phones and need to get pictures or maybe even try and grab some kind of real evidence. If they're hiding what

I think they are, it doesn't belong to them anyway."

Andrea thought about the mini documentary Seth had let her watch earlier. If that conspiracy theory was even close to being accurate, then Seth was right. She wasn't sure just who the cave's contents belonged to, but it wasn't any government or military group. Finally, she nodded. "Okay, we'll try your surveillance idea. What if we don't see anyone heading from one cave to another though? How long do you plan on staying out here and watching?"

Seth shrugged. "A few hours at the most. The only food we brought along was a couple of protein bars. They won't last long. If we find that cave though, I promise I'll buy you dinner at any place you choose. How's that sound?"

Andrea stuck out her hand and when Seth took it, she shook it firmly up and down. "You have yourself a deal."

Seth smiled. "Great, are you ready to start hiking?"

Andrea nodded. "You lead, I'll follow."

The two took off walking. Andrea, by now, had lost all sense of direction. When she mentioned that fact to Seth he laughed. "You just need to watch the sun. As long as I can remember it has always set in the west. I think we can trust it to continue the pattern."

Andrea slugged Seth's shoulder. "You're really funny Seth, you should be a comedian."

Playfully rubbing his shoulder, Seth flashed Andrea a smile. "I have my moments."

The two continued their hike. As they ducked under trees and pushed aside bushes, Andrea hoped that all of this would be worth it and they'd actually uncover a hidden conspiracy.

Tripping on a rock and stumbling into Seth,

she thought about Mel and hoped her friend was having a better day than she was. Realizing that Mel's better days were going to be a long way in the future, Andrea felt guilty for making the comparison. A few scratches were nothing compared to what happened to Mel.

Seth looked back at his friend. "Are you doing okay?"

Andrea nodded. "I'm fine, how much further?"

Seth stopped walking. "Let's take a break." He pointed over at a couple of rocks. "Sit down and rest a minute. Just up ahead is the base of the hill I want to watch from. We'll have to hike up at least half way up in order to get a good vantage point. It's a little bit steeper than some around here, but the hike isn't all that bad."

Andrea sat down and taking off her shoes, rubbed her feet before slipping her sneakers back on, then sighing. "Oh wow, that's much better, I didn't realize how bad of shape I was in. You'd think I'd be used to it. I usually stand on my feet all day at the factory, but that's nothing compared to hiking."

Seth shook his head. "I think you're holding up pretty well. I'm not used to hiking either. Maybe in my younger days, but now I spend too much time on the couch watching old movies."

Andrea smiled. "After this, I think you better cut back on those detective shows."

Seth grinned. "Now who's the comedian?" Slipping off his pack, Seth pulled out two bottles of water and a couple of protein bars. He handed one of each to Andrea before putting his pack back on. The two sat in silence as they took in the nourishment. When they finished, Seth placed the garbage in his pack and then stood. "C'mon, I think we better get moving."

Sighing, Andrea stood up and nodded that she was ready. It didn't take long for them to reach the base of the hill that Seth had talked about. Leaning her head back, Andrea stared up at the hill. She was thinking it looked more like Mount Everest to her than the hill Seth kept calling it. She hoped she was up for the hike so she didn't impede Seth's journey. At the same time, she knew there was no stopping her from needing to be part of that journey. She had gotten a glimpse of too much and now had to see the rest, no matter what. Andrea knew she'd come too far to turn back now and took a deep breath as she straightened her shoulders. A picture of Mel lying in the hospital bed, her leg in a cast, flashed through Andrea's mind. No matter what it took, Andrea knew she had to do this for her friend. Mel would have loved to be here with them looking for a conspiracy and Andrea couldn't wait until they got back so she could share it all with her friend.

Seeing the look of doubt on her face when she had looked up at the hill, Seth gave Andrea an encouraging smile. "It's easier than it looks. You'll do fine."

As the two made their way up the side of the large hill, Andrea found herself crawling on hands and knees more often than not. At first when she had to drop down on all fours, she felt like some kind of wimp for doing that, but knowing she was safer closer to the ground replaced the feeling of inadequacy. Instead after a short time, she congratulated herself on just keeping up with Seth. Andrea envied Seth. Who looked like he was able to climb up the hillside like he was part mountain goat or some other four legged creature that also happened to climb mountains.

Andrea was just happy when Seth pointed at a spot under a tree and announced that would be where they would set up their observation post.

The two removed their backpacks and took out their binoculars, some water and another protein bar. Seth unwrapped his quickly and almost devoured the whole bar before Andrea finished chewing her first bite. She smiled. "There's a few more left if you want another."

Seth shook his head as he lifted his binoculars and adjusted them. "I'll be okay, at least for a minute or two."

Shaking her head, Andrea finished her snack and took a moment to look around.
The area around her was beautiful and she was reminded of her thoughts of the other morning about spending time in the woods being an almost spiritual experience.
Realizing that had barely been two days ago, Andrea shook her head, it felt like all that had happened an eternity ago.
Still, right now she felt at peace looking at the leaves that had just begun to change colors. The vibrant hues of yellow and orange seemed to stand out in brilliant

contrast against the green of the pine trees and set off by the cerulean sky. Off to one side the sapphire color of the lake seemed to vie for her attention. There was a stillness in the air though that seemed sad to Andrea. She longed for the sound of people. There should be families over in the campground or people out in their boats on the lake. Instead the place had been shut down and sealed off. These people, whoever they were, had robbed that happiness and Andrea felt the emptiness deep in her soul.

As she felt Seth staring, she turned to him, the hurt evident in her eyes.

Seth was frowning. "Are you okay?"

Andrea shrugged. "It's too quiet. This place was made for enjoying, not being closed down so a group of people can hide their damn secrets."

Seth nodded. "You're right, and that's exactly why we're up here. I feel the same way you do and if these people are hiding what we think they are, that secret is one that needs to be revealed and then shared with the world."

Andrea nodded. "I've been thinking about that since I watched that story on your laptop. I think I remember seeing a show on TV a few years back about something similar. What I don't understand is why? I mean why hide something like that? If what we think is hidden in a cave or two around here, wouldn't it be worth a fortune? You'd think they'd be trying to make a profit by bringing out what they have. Although they have no right to any of the proceeds from it. I bet a museum would pay a lot of money for something like that though."

Seth nodded. "You're right, but who would be the rightful owner of their secrets? I think they probably have sold part of what they stole. They would have to be careful, because they know if the public found out about what is hidden they would want it returned where it was taken from. According to that documentary, this was a vast conspiracy and one that may be spread out all over not just here in America, but other countries as well. I think through the years, some of the pieces have been sold to private collectors. Think about it, that necklace I found is worth thousands of dollars. What must the rest of the stolen property be worth?"

Andrea frowned. "But the majority of the people it was taken from are most likely dead by now."

Seth nodded. "I agree, but I think their relative's should have the right to decide what should be done with that treasure. Either that or like you said, it should be placed in a museum."

Nodding, Andrea then sighed. "If it's even here, if we can get proof and if we can find a way to expose these people. That's a whole lot of ifs."

Andrea was quiet a moment, thinking back

to the horrific time, so many years ago, when all this had started and to those who had been behind the atrocity. She was about to mention that to Seth when he pointed and lifted his binoculars.

"Someone's coming out of the cave."

Andrea lifted her own binoculars to take a look at the area that Seth was observing and at the man who had stepped out of the cave. "Oh hell, look at all the medals on that guys' uniform."

Seth nodded. "He must be some kind of General. That's the guy we need to follow."

The two watched as the General talked to two other men who had followed him out of the cave. Seth wished he could hear what they were saying. A moment later, as Seth and Andrea watched, one of the men turned and walked back into the cave. The General, accompanied by the other man, walked away from the cave entrance.

Seth grabbed his pack, threw the empty water bottle and the wrapper in it and then put the pack on. He turned to Andrea. "Hurry and grab your stuff, we need to keep an eye on those two. Follow me, but stay low. We don't want to take any chances on them seeing us."

Andrea nodded as she nervously did what Seth had told her to. She could feel her heart racing and knew that was ridiculous. This adventure was only just beginning.

Half way down the hill, Seth motioned with his hand for Andrea to get down. Since she'd been sliding on her backside down the hill anyway, it wasn't a far drop to the ground for her. In fact, she'd just been thinking how terrible it would be if the seat on her jeans ripped with all the stress she was putting on it while sliding on her butt over the rocks.

Seth pointed down the hill and slightly to the left. "They're headed into a cave."

A moment later, Seth half stood and grabbed Andrea's hand. "We need to move. I'll help you the rest of the way."

Andrea nodded gratefully and let Seth half pull her down to the bottom of the hill. As soon as they got there, Seth turned to Andrea and whispered. "The entrance is only about twenty yards away. I want to head through the woods and make a circle so we can get behind that hill with the cave. Maybe we'll get lucky and find a back way in. Then we can see what's really going on around here."

Andrea nodded as she answered back, her voice quiet also. "You just lead the way. You know this place better than I do. Don't worry about me, I'll only be one step behind you."

Walking through the woods, the two eventually circled around, coming up behind the hill. Seth started pushing aside bushes looking for a tunnel. Seeing what he was doing, Andrea followed suit. Spotting a large rock, she grunted as she pushed on the rock, but was only able to move it a few inches. Looking behind the rock, Andrea could see loose dirt piled behind it.

Not wanting to yell out, Andrea instead quickly walked over to Seth and spoke in a low voice. "I think I found something, but I can't move the damn rock." Andrea pointed back at the rock.

Nodding, Seth walked over and pushed the rock further away from the hill. Andrea stepped over and began scooping away the loosened dirt. She smiled broadly as a hole appeared. Seth grinned and whispered. "Great work Andrea. I think this might be just what we're looking for."

Seth joined Andrea and the two began pushing away the dirt and rocks until a hole big enough to crawl through was made.

Andrea looked at the hole and a shiver ran up her spine as she wondered how many creepy crawlies would be inside. She pointed at Seth. "You can go first."

Seeing the disgusted look on her face, Seth nodded. Slipping off his pack, he pulled out his flashlight, put his pack back on and got down on the ground so he could squirm into the hole. As soon as his feet cleared the entrance, Andrea quickly followed, not liking standing out in the open all alone. By the time she made it inside, Seth was already standing and using his flashlight to look around. The tunnel split just a few feet from where they were standing. Seth pointed to the left and spoke quietly. "Since we're on the backside of the cave, I think we should go that way. It should take us back the way we came and hopefully to the backside of that cave the General went in."

Andrea shrugged, when she spoke, her voice came out in a whisper. "Your judgment is better than mine, I just feel like we've been going in circles."

Seth laughed softly. "We almost have. C'mon let's go see what we can find."

With Seth leading the way, the two had only gone about ten feet into the tunnel when they heard the murmuring of voices. Andrea felt her heart skip a beat in anticipation.
Seth placed his hands on the tunnel walls, feeling for loose dirt. If his brothers and he learned anything exploring this area as kids, it was that a lot of the walls were weak and could easily be pushed through. He was glad now they had spent so much time playing explorers when they were growing up and spending summers at the cabin.
As each piece of dirt crumbled off, Seth would dig carefully, trying to make a hole small enough to peek through. Finally after a half a dozen tries, a thin beam of light could be seen coming through. Making a circle with his fingers, Seth put it against the hole

he'd made and then leaned so his eye was up against his curled up fingers. He took a breath and held it as he looked from one side of the room to the other. Stepping back, he let out his breath, shaking his head in wonder. Then he moved aside to let Andrea repeat the procedure he'd used.
Looking through, it took all the self-control Andrea had not to scream in astonishment. The room was filled with a variety of treasures. The cave not only had bins that appeared to be filled with gold and jewels, but against one wall, Andrea could see several ornate frames holding beautiful pieces of artwork.

Stepping back, Andrea stared wide eyed at Seth. Her voice came out in a high pitched whisper. "What the hell is all that? Do you really think that treasure could be what the documentary claimed it is?"

Seth was about to answer when he heard a sound and stared at the two guards who appeared in the tunnel, one holding a handgun and the other a rifle. One of the men shouted at them. "Don't move, this is private property and both of you are trespassing."

Seth took a step toward the man with the rifle, not noticing as the other guard stepped swiftly over to Andrea. Wrapping an arm around her, the man pulled her close and put his pistol to Andrea's head. "Hold it right there, one more step and your little friend's brains are going to be splattered all over this tunnel."

Seth stopped, his shoulders drooping in defeat. "Take it easy, I'm not moving. Just take your gun off her. We didn't know anyone was in here. We were just up here hiking and got lost."

Andrea wanted to nod her head in agreement, but instead she was frozen in place, waiting to see if the guard would withdraw his gun. The guard with the rifle pointed at Seth, pulled out a set of handcuffs. "We'll see about that. Right now, you two are coming with us. Put your hands behind your back."

Seth did as he was told, sure that neither of these two would even think twice about shooting anyone who had seen what they were hiding.

As soon as Seth was handcuffed, the gun that had been pressed against Andrea's temple was pulled back and the blond haired man holding her released his grip so he too could pull out a set of handcuffs. Moving the gun that had been pressed against Andrea's head, the man pointed it to a place not too far from her heart. The man then waved the pistol, motioning it in a circle. "Now you, turn around and put your arms behind your back."

After Andrea was handcuffed, the man grabbed her roughly by the elbow and pulled her behind him.

The other, darker haired guard, who looked a few years older than the one manhandling Andrea, did the same with Seth and the two friends were escorted out of the tunnel. A few minutes later, Seth and Andrea were pushed roughly into the larger cave.

Seth was more than a little surprised that they had been brought to the room with its' secret treasures, then worried. This group didn't want any witnesses to what they were hiding. That meant they also had plans for getting rid of those witnesses. Trying not to think what that meant for him and Andrea, Seth focused his attention on the General.

Andrea was instead paying more attention to the large picture the General was standing in front of. The artwork was at least six feet high and four feet wide. It was a beautiful landscape, and one Andrea knew had to be stolen, just like all the other treasures in the room. If the documentary was accurate, during World War Two, it had taken Hitler and his cohorts several years to accumulate the vast stolen treasure and then move it to various secret locations around the world. Andrea was certain this cave they were in now, held at least part of that treasure.

The guards moved Seth and Andrea to the far corner of the room where two heavy metal chairs sat. The pair were pushed down onto the chairs and then fastened to the seats before the guards stepped back and faced the General. Both stood straight and stiff, at attention. The General's steel blue eyes were hard as he stared at the men. Turning to the younger man, the General pointed a finger toward the cave entrance. "Corporal Vaugn, I want you to guard the front of this cave."

The General turned to the other man. "Corporal Weston, I want you to find a crew of a dozen men, have them scour this area. Check for any trespassers. You better hope to hell they don't find any. I don't know how anyone in their right mind let these two get past. I do know that someone's ass is going to be in a sling for letting it happen."

Hearing the General's words, Seth struggled against his restraints. "We're not trespassing. This happens to be public land."

The General turned to glare at Seth. "Not now it isn't. This whole place was quarantined."

Seth glanced quickly at Andrea then turned back to the General. "We were camping and had been up hiking, we didn't hear anything about a quarantine."

Seth then looked around the room. "I don't see anything dangerous or toxic in here. Why should Hidden Lake be under quarantine anyway, what's going on up here?"

The General shook his head. "You let me worry about that. The two of you are in enough trouble."

The General looked at Corporal Weston. "I think you have your orders."

Nodding, the corporal saluted. "Yes sir, I'm on that sir." Then he hurried out of the cave.

Corporal Vaugn also saluted and started to turn away when the General stopped him. "Before you take up your position, I need you to go find Lieutenant Franklin and inform him I need him to bring the trucks over here. We have a lot of work to do and quickly. He knows what is needed. Just tell him he has the green light for operation 'Relegate', he'll handle the rest."

Corporal Vaugn saluted again. "I'll take care of it sir."

The General returned the salute before turning back to where Seth and Andrea were secured to the chairs.
"There has been a toxic spill in this area, no matter what you think. I'm afraid the two of you have been exposed. I'm going to have

you taken to the veteran's hospital in Monarch. It's an hour from Hagen Falls, but the VA hospital is more qualified than the hospital they have in Hagen Falls."

Andrea shook her head, angry that they were being lied to. "We didn't see any toxic spill and both of us feel fine. What the hell is going on here? What's all this stuff in this cave? Just what are you hiding?"

The glare Andrea received made her cringe and lean back in her chair. The General stepped toward her. "You're in no position to ask questions young lady. In fact, you may find things will go a lot easier if you remember the old adage 'silence is golden'. When your transportation arrives, the two of you will be taken out of here and to the hospital to be looked at. If your tests turn out okay and your story checks out, we can see about your release."

Seth looked at the General and tried to keep a blank look on his face. Because he was certain they wouldn't be released, that was a hard feat to accomplish. He, like Andrea, knew their health was fine and there wasn't any way for the General to find out what they had been doing up here and why.

The fact that they had been allowed in this cave with its' hidden secrets, confirmed the truth to Seth. There was no way they would be let go. The two of them had seen too much. Even if they wouldn't have had an idea as to what was really going on here or where the treasure had originally come from, now their lives were in danger.

It had been since the moment they had been caught and brought to the General's attention inside the cave with its' hidden secrets.

All Seth could do at the moment, was pray he could find a way for him and Andrea to stay alive until they could escape. He hoped they would find an option for escape at this hospital the General said they were being taken to. If they couldn't, Seth was afraid there would be no way out of this predicament that would be in their favor.

Chapter 7

Before either Seth or Andrea had much time to dwell on their predicament, they could hear the sound of the engines of several large trucks pulling up outside the cave. The General, knowing his prisoners were not only secured to the chairs, but also handcuffed, turned his attention to the forty something man who stepped just to the very edge of the cave entrance.

Watching the General and the other man, also in military attire, Seth figured this must be the Lieutenant Franklin who the General had talked about and who was in charge of operation 'Relegate', whatever that was. Seth had an idea it meant they were moving the treasure. Probably to another spot similar to Hidden Lake. According to the documentary, during World War Two,

Hitler had ordered vast amounts of treasures stolen during the atrocity of the Holocaust to secretly be relocated. Hitler, it seemed had a passion for areas with lakes and various locations had been chosen around the globe. Artwork and jewelry, especially anything containing gold and other precious metals had been taken. Seth had been appalled to learn, from the documentary, that the stolen treasure even included victims' gold teeth as they entered the concentration camps. Seth shuddered at that last thought. Those poor people had endured so much. To not only be taken to those awful camps, where too many atrocities had been allowed to happen, but to have the teeth ripped from your mouth, and most certainly without any kind of anesthetic. He didn't know how the people who lived through the atrocity, didn't come out of it bitter and ready for some kind of revenge. Now, in a strange twist of fate, the U.S. military had somehow become owners of that ill-gotten treasure stolen from them. Seth turned to Andrea, who was staring wide eyed around the room. He knew her thoughts had to be similar to his own. Leaning toward her as far as the restraints would allow, Seth spoke quietly. "Andrea, these guys aren't just going to let us go. We've seen too much. Even if we didn't know about the Hitler connection, they aren't going to risk our telling about what we saw here. I can only think they plan on moving everything, now that we laid eyes on it. If they take us to the veteran's hospital, like they said, we shouldn't be under such tight scrutiny and that is going to be the best place for us to make an escape."

Andrea frowned. "The day after tomorrow is Tuesday. Both of us are supposed to be back at work then, what if someone comes looking for us when we don't show up? I'm sure Mel will figure out that we decided to come back up here. She knew we might come get your truck, it wouldn't take much for her to figure out we went looking for that spaceship. She doesn't even know this half of the story, but she knows enough to point someone in this area."

Andrea thought of her cell phone, it was in her backpack laying in the bottom of her purse. "I wish I could get to my phone."

Seth nodded. "My cell's in my pack too, but I wouldn't want to endanger anyone calling for help. We're on our own Andrea. Don't worry, we'll find a way out of this."

Before Andrea could answer, the General turned and walked back to them. "The two of you are being transported to the hospital. You'll be checked out medically once you get there and a full investigation will also have to be done. With the Hidden Lake area closed off, you are trespassers on a military operation and will be treated as such."

Shaking his head, Seth frowned. "What's the military have to do with this place anyway? Shouldn't the Forest Service be the ones blocking off the area, if it even needed closed off that is?"

The General bent down so his face was only a few inches from Seth's' own. "I suggest you keep that big mouth of yours shut. It's people like you who are ruining this country. You don't need to ask for more trouble than you're already in."

Seth couldn't help but think the General's tone might be different if he wasn't handcuffed to the chair right now. Then again, although Seth considered himself to be in good shape, the General did look intimidating and Seth had to admit in better shape. The gun nestled in the holster on the General's hip was also in the man's favor.

The General maintained his steely glare a moment before stepping back as the two guards, who had captured Seth and Andrea, stepped in the room. Moving closer, the two stood at attention as they saluted the General. Returning the salute, General Corbin then turned and pointed at Seth and Andrea. "I want these two taken straight to the VA hospital. The two of you are to

151

remain in their presence at all times, is that understood?"

The "yes sirs" came in unison and Stan Corbin nodded. "Good, I don't want any screw ups, I'll be in touch after my other business here is taken care of. Have these two checked out. There's no time now, but when you get to the hospital, I also want you to find their ID's and call me with that information." The General scowled at the soldiers when they didn't move immediately. "I said I want them out of here right now, before I begin operation 'Relocation'."

Seth and Andrea were each grabbed by one of the Corporals and yanked to a standing position. The two were taken outside where a military SUV was waiting and thrown roughly into the back seat. The first thing Seth noticed, was the absence of door handles.

He'd been picked up once in his college days for being part of a fight in a bar. The

whole thing had started out as a small
argument and gotten quickly out of hand.
Before he knew it, the whole bar seemed to
have joined in and become part of the brawl.
Several people had been handcuffed and
thrown in the two police cars and the one
wagon that had shown up. The police car
Seth had been taken to the station in had
been built the same way as this military
SUV. Seth knew for sure now that their best
chance of escape would have to be from the
hospital they were being escorted to.
Seeing the look of worry and fear on
Andrea's face, Seth tried to give her a
reassuring look. He longed to grab her hand
and hold it and wished their hands weren't
fastened behind them. Not only was it
uncomfortable to be secured this way, but
the two corporals hadn't bothered to remove
the backpacks he and Andrea still wore. Seth
imagined that was because they were in such
a hurry to get their two witnesses away from
the cave before they were able to see any
more of what was hidden there, or in which

direction they went as they began operation 'Relocate' and moved the treasure.

Now, both Andrea and Seth had to not only sit forward on their seats, but lean ahead to avoid the bulk of the packs pushing against their backs.

The hour long drive to Monarch was taken in silence by Seth and Andrea. Both of them were afraid to speak with the two military men in the front seat, who were easily able to hear anything the two friends said. Just like they could, in turn, hear the men. In fact, Seth was listening closely, hoping to catch word of anything about the treasures he knew were being moved from the cave.

The driver, who looked to be the older of the two, but not by much, was the first to speak. "We really lucked out Clark. I'd hate to be stuck back at the lake. Corbin's going to tear those guys a new asshole for allowing these two in the cave."

Clark nodded. "It's going to be hell on someone alright. I'm glad we found them and weren't the ones on guard. I don't think we're off the hook yet though. After we finish at the hospital, I'm sure we'll get an ear full too. Shit Gary, maybe the General has the right to be pissed. With all of us on duty up there, I still don't see how these two snuck into that cave."

Gary shrugged. "Maybe they really were camping and got lost."

Looking in his rearview mirror, Gary was able to see Andrea. The pale face made her blue eyes stand out and they looked terrified to Gary. He almost felt sorry for her. Maybe if she had been alone he would have, but the guy she was with looked like he could take care of himself. Gary had a feeling they both knew exactly what they were doing when they had entered the tunnel into the cave. He shook his head not wanting to think about any of that and changed the subject. "Hey

Clark, who do you think is going to win the World Series this year?"

Glad for the change of subject, Clark gladly talked baseball until Gary pulled into the parking lot behind the VA Hospital.

As soon as they brought their prisoners in, they were greeted and ushered quickly to a room where a Doctor and a nurse stood waiting. Seeing them standing there, not only the Corporals, but Seth and Andrea knew that General Corbin had to be behind the emergency treatment they were receiving.

The first thing the Doctor did was request that the corporals remove the handcuffs that were on Seth and Andrea wrists and then that their backpacks be removed. Gary took the packs, berating himself for not taking them earlier. General Corbin said there would be an investigation of the two and Gary Weston knew it was up to him to identify the prisoners for a security check and report back to the General. Now that would have to wait so it could be done in private. He wasn't sure what story the General had told the Doctor and didn't want to risk pulling something incriminating out of the packs in front of the man.

The room they had been brought to, held two hospital beds and the Doctor, after taking Seth and Andrea's names, had Seth sit on one bed and Andrea on the other. He began by examining Seth, while the nurse who had come in the room with them got busy taking Andrea's temperature and blood pressure. She was talking quietly to Andrea as she went about her work.

"Now don't you worry. We're going to get you fixed up. My name is Sherry and this is Doctor Paulson. You're both lucky, he's the absolute best."

Andrea sighed, she was tired, scared and more than a little angry. "There's nothing wrong with me or Seth either. These goons and their boss arrested us on made up charges. We shouldn't even be here, this is all a mistake."

The nurse reached over to touch Andrea's shoulder. "Getting upset won't help. I have nothing to do with how you were transported here. My concern is for your health. You might feel fine right now, but believe me that can change quickly. You just need to try and relax. We'll take care of everything."

Andrea looked over at where Seth was being examined just a few feet away. He tried to give her what he hoped was a warning look, and hoping she understood why. General Corbin had surely talked to this Doctor and nothing he or Andrea said would override the General's orders. Instead of talking, Seth looked around the room, hoping to find a way to escape, while trying to stay inconspicuous.

The Doctor, seeing the guards had taken seats in the room's two chairs frowned. "I think it would be best if both of you waited outside the door. These patients aren't going anywhere and I have the feeling your presence is making them nervous."

Without saying a word, Gary walked into the adjoining bathroom. Looking around, he made sure the room didn't hold any doors or windows that would make an easy escape. Satisfied the prisoners were secure, he returned to the main room, and stepped over to where Clark still sat. "C'mon, we can go out in the hall, this door is the only way out."

Gary turned to glare at the prisoners before he turned to the Doctor and his nurse. "We'll be just outside the door."

The two walked out and the Doctor resumed his examination. He'd received a frantic call and firm instructions from General Corbin that these two were to remain in the hospital until the General himself could get here. Which the General said wouldn't be until in the morning. James Paulson was a Doctor, and he hoped a good one, but he was also an employee of the veteran's administration and knew he had no choice but to do as the General had ordered, like it or not.

Going from Seth to Andrea, the Doctor also examined her. When he finished, he turned to Sherry. "Nurse Johnson, these two have been exposed to toxic chemicals. I'm afraid there may be a delayed reaction. I need you to go to the front desk and admit both of them as patients. While you're at it, do you think we could get these two something to eat? I'm sure they must be hungry."

Nodding at the Doctor, Sherry then turned to Seth and Andrea. "I'll have to have your ID's and also I need to make a copy of an insurance card if you have one."

Seth reached for his wallet, but Andrea frowned. "My purse is in the backpack those guards took. I don't understand why you need our insurance cards though. If anything is wrong, which I am sure there isn't, the military should be the one that has to foot the bill."

Andrea knew that she and Seth hadn't been exposed to anything more than the General's lies. She also knew she and Seth would be better off if she didn't voice her opinion any more than she already had.

Sherry nodded at Andrea. "Of course you won't be the ones responsible for the bill, it's just standard procedure. Let me go and get your purse for you."

Sherry went out to the hall. She saw the blonde corporal in the chair, but his darker haired companion was absent. She spoke to Corporal Vaughn. "I need to get the young lady's purse. She said it's in her backpack. Do you have it?"

Clark Vaughn frowned. "No, Corporal Weston has the packs. He'll be back in a minute though."

Nodding, Sherry folded her arms, and then stood in the hall, frowning at the man and waiting.

Corporal Weston had found Andrea's ID when he searched her backpack and was calling the information into the General. He wished he had gotten both prisoners' ID's. He hated calling the General with only half the information and knowing that he was going to have to make a second call.

After finishing his call to the General, Gary returned to find Sherry standing by Clark and not looking too happy. She glared at Gary as he walked up. "If you're done, I need the purse that's in one of those backpacks. I believe it belongs to Miss Larson."

Thankful he'd already replaced Andrea's driver's license back in her wallet, Gary reached in the backpack and pulled out the purse. Without a thank you, Sherry took the purse and hurried back into the hospital room. Stepping over to Andrea, she gave her the purse. Sherry waited for the woman to retrieve her license and insurance card. Taking Seth's from him also, Sherry smiled. "This shouldn't take too long, I'll just make copies and get these right back to you."

As Sherry stepped in the hall, she gave the two guards a disgusted look. She didn't care for the two of them being here. The guns on their hips only escalated her disgust.

The guard with the dark hair frowned as he saw the ID's Sherry held in her hand. He pointed at the cards. "What are you doing with those?"

Sherry's forehead creased in disapproval. "If it's any of your business, I'm making copies for our records."

Gary Weston stood and glared down at the much shorter Sherry. "I'm afraid I am going to have to take a look at those."

Sherry pulled her hand, clutching the ID's, close to her chest. "Wait a minute, I was given these in good faith. I don't believe your name came up in the deal."

Gary scowled at Sherry. "Listen, I have to do my job, just like everyone else. No one knows who those two really are, or why they just happened to show up right after a chemical explosion. This is a matter for National Security. I don't think you want to be given orders by someone with more seniority than me to let me have a look at those."

Reluctantly, Sherry handed over the ID's, feeling she didn't have much choice in the matter.

Gary pulled a small notebook and pen from his pocket and copied the information from both ID's. He already had Andrea's information, but didn't want this nurse, who to Gary, was being a bitch, to know he had dug through Andrea's purse earlier.

As soon as Gary handed back the ID's, Sherry turned and stomped off.

Going to the cafeteria, she asked for food trays to be brought to the hospitals two newest patients. She could have made up the trays and delivered them herself, but right now, she didn't feel she could face either Seth or Andrea. That guard had made her feel that by getting the information, she was not only a thief of their identities, but somehow putting them in danger. Instead, Sherry headed to the Administration Office to put the finishing touches on the pairs' admittance.

While Sherry was busy doing her work, back in the hospital room, Doctor Paulson turned to look at his two patients. "I'm going to have a nurse come in and draw some blood. I'll try to put a rush on the results. I'm going to let the two of you stay together in this room. I'm sure that will make your guards happy. Easier to keep an eye on you that way. I'll be back as soon as I can. Sherry should be back soon. We've just finished serving dinner, but I know she will be able to rustle you up something and have it brought back."

James didn't wait for an answer or to hear any objections as he turned and left the room.

Stepping out in the hall, James only saw one of the guards. "Did your partner leave?"

Clark shook his head. "Gary just went to make a call." Clark pointed at the door. "What's the verdict on those two?"

James didn't like this man or the other one with him. He also didn't like following the orders he was given, but he was a realist and knew there was no changing anything about this situation. "They'll be here overnight for observation. Your boss is supposed to be here in the morning. So you'll know, I'll be having a nurse come up here to draw some blood and someone is going to be bringing those two up some dinner. Don't worry, I'll make sure they have on their hospital ID tags. I'd appreciate it if you don't bother them or stop them for doing their duty. This place is first and foremost a hospital. I hope you will remember that."

Clark held up his hands. "Gary and I are just doing our duty too. As long as those two stay in their room, we won't have a problem."

James nodded. "That's all I ask."

The Doctor walked away, worried and angry about the predicament he found himself in.

*

In the hospital room, still sitting on the bed he had been given, Seth jumped up and walked over to where Andrea was seated on her own bed and digging through her purse. "Damn, it's not here, those bastards took my cell phone. They had no right to dig through my purse."

Taking a seat next to Andrea, Seth patted her leg. "It's okay, I don't think making a call to anyone would help us anyway."

Andrea nodded and then sighed. "It's not about making a call, although I would love to check in with my grandma. Not to tell her what's going on, but just so she won't call first, not reach me, and worry. It's about invasion of our privacy. I know we're supposed to be under some kind of military arrest, but this is all just wrong. That General and his people, they were the ones breaking the law, not us."
Shaking her head, Andrea stared at Seth. "What are they going to do to us?"

Reaching his arms around Andrea, Seth pulled her close and hugged her. "They aren't going to do anything. We're going to find a way to get out of here. We just have to watch for the right moment and then act on it. You just make sure you're ready for a fast escape when that time comes."

Outside the room, Gary returned from making his second call to the General, after getting the information from Seth's ID that Sherry had. He had taken time to think about the attitude the nurse had pulled on him and now had second thoughts about thinking she was being bitchy. He hated doing what he was also. He also knew he had no other choice in the matter.

Gary took the seat next to Clark. "General Corbin has the information on those two now. He said he'll be here in the morning after he runs the checks on them. The General also said he was bringing another Doctor with him to take over the treatment of those two."

Clark stared at Gary, his blue eyes squinted in disbelief. "Doctor Paulson isn't going to like that. He's already pissed off that we're here. What in the hell is he going to say when Corbin takes him off the cases and puts this other Doctor in charge?"

Gary shrugged. "I really don't care what he says. The good Doctor takes his orders just like we do. I don't like arresting a couple of people and bringing them here, but I do what I'm told to do. Just forget about it. What I'm more worried about right now is getting us something to eat. Do you think we can get some food around here?"

Clark nodded. "The Doctor said he was having a couple of trays brought up to our prisoners. I'm sure we can get something."

Gary rubbed his hands together. "Great, why don't you check on that? I had to make those calls to the General. It's your turn to do the running."

Clark stood up. "Of the two jobs, I like getting us a meal a lot better than talking to Corbin. I'll be back as soon as I can."

Gary leaned back in his chair, stretched his legs out in front of him and then crossed his ankles and folded his arms. He felt like from the time him and Clark had found the prisoners until know was more like days not hours and he was totally worn out.

A few minutes later, a male nurse pushing a cart had Gary looking up as the nurse stopped next to him. "I have orders to draw some blood. Doctor Paulson said to make sure and show you my hospital I.D." The man unclipped his badge and handed it to Gary. As the corporal looked at the man's badge, a young woman, also pushing a cart, stepped up beside the two. She smiled at the men. "Just bringing some dinner."

Gary handed the man's badge back and took the one the woman offered. He could smell the food and his stomach growled. Giving the woman back her badge, Gary nodded. "You're both okay to go in."

As the two closed the door behind them, Gary sat up in his chair, eagerly awaiting Clark's return with their own dinner.

In the hospital room, Seth and Andrea were once again on their own beds, the male nurse explained he'd be drawing blood and then quickly went about his job. As soon as he finished he left the room.

The young woman placed the food trays on the stands that sat by the beds. She stared at the two new patients. Already rumors had spread through the hospital about this pair. Everyone knew their admittance orders had come from General Corbin. Because he was military, they knew none of them were supposed to talk about the patients. That knowledge didn't go far in stopping the speculations that were flying around. If anything, it seemed to only increase the talk. The woman smiled at the two patients. "Just to let you know, my name is Misty. Sherry asked for us to bring you up a food tray. She forgot to ask the two of you what you wanted, but she was worried you'd say you weren't hungry and refuse food anyway. So you get what Sherry requested, if you want anything different, or if this isn't enough, just ring your buzzers. We can always bring you a drink or dessert. As far as I know, we haven't been notified of any food restrictions, so if we have it on hand, it's yours."

Looking at her tray of food, Andrea didn't feel like she could eat anything right now. She gave Misty a slight smile and shook her head. "I think this is plenty. Thanks for bringing it in."

Misty shrugged. "No problem, remember, just push your buzzers if you need anything."

Misty left the room. She wished she could have stayed and found out a little bit more about the patients, but neither had seemed too talkative. At least she had memorized their descriptions. That put her one up on the rest of the hospital rumor mill anyway.

As soon as the door shut behind the woman, Andrea turned to stare at Seth who had already started eating. "What are you doing

Seth, are you sure it's safe to eat that? They could have drugged it or something."

Seth shrugged. "I think we're okay. I don't think they had time to set anything up yet. Besides, I'm starving, aren't you?"

Andrea shook her head. "Not really, I just want out of here. I wish we'd never heard about the Nazi's hidden treasure."

Seth frowned, his brown eyes sad. "I'm really sorry I got you into this. I mean it Andrea, I didn't expect any of this to happen. I should have known better and I never should have brought you into my crazy idea of going back to Hidden Lake."

The blue eyes staring at Seth narrowed. "There's nothing to be sorry for. I wanted to come up here. Maybe even more than you did. The story was so intriguing and the thought that it all was happening right there at Hidden Lake was too much to not want to investigate. You need to stop apologizing

Seth. I mean that, let's just focus on getting out of this place."

Seth smiled. "You're right, I won't do it anymore. Now eat some of your dinner. We both need to keep up our strength."

Even though she wasn't as sure as Seth about the safety of the food or whether or not it would help keep up her strength, Andrea picked at her plate until she had eaten a small part of her meal.

An hour later, a nurse came back in the room to gather up their trays. She brought both Seth and Andrea's ID's and insurance cards. Telling them Sherry had gotten busy but wanted to make sure the cards were returned. The nurse had been followed in by Doctor Paulson. As soon as she left the room, the Doctor addressed both Seth and Andrea. "I'm afraid we'll be waiting until morning for those test results. I wanted to give you some kind of news tonight, but these things take time. In the meantime, I want both of you to get some rest. If either of you start to have any physical problems, I don't care how trivial they seem, I want you to buzz the nurse immediately. Something that seems minor can turn into something serious quicker than you can imagine, so if there is anything, we need to know about it right away. I'm headed home for the night, but I have left word for the nurses to call me if anything happens and you need me."

Both Andrea and Seth nodded that they understood the Doctor's instructions, but then Andrea frowned. "You can't possibly think there's actually anything wrong with us. We weren't exposed to anything up at Hidden Lake. We really are both feeling fine and I don't think that will change. I wish you'd just release us."

The Doctor shook his head. "Even if I did release you from the hospital, you're both still under General Corbin's custody. I'd think being here is much better than the alternative he'd have for you both."

Seth let out a sigh. "He's got a good point Andrea. Thanks for reminding us of that Doctor Paulson."

Nodding, the Doctor smiled. "You're welcome and you can call me James. Now, get some sleep. I'll be here first thing in the morning and then we'll see what those tests say."

As the Doctor left the room, he couldn't help but wonder what excuse the General would come up with to keep those two as prisoners when the tests came back negative. He knew there would be something. Corbin wasn't going to just let them walk out of the hospital and go free. James didn't know what the General was doing up at the lake, but he knew that what Andrea had said was true...There had been no toxic exposure.

As he headed out of the hospital and drove home, James knew he wasn't going to be able to get any sleep tonight for worrying about it either.

*

In their hospital room, Seth and Andrea were both in the beds with their clothes on after refusing offers for hospital gowns. Both had laughed at the thought of wearing the gowns. Neither wanted to take the chance of having their asses exposed if they found a chance for escape and had to make a run for it during the night.

The two talked about everything except the treasure they had seen in the cave at Hidden Lake. Finally, they drifted off into a restless sleep, while outside their door, Clark and Gary tried to get comfortable for what they knew would be a long night.

*

At a makeshift office, thirty minutes from Hidden Lake, General Corbin leaned back in his chair. They'd been able to move not only most of the cave's treasure but the spaceship they used as a distraction, to this new location. The place wasn't far from Hidden Lake, but it was more remote. Stan Corbin hoped it would be secluded enough to keep out people like Seth Reynolds and Andrea Larson.

He thought he'd finally come up with the only viable plan for his two prisoners. Picking up his phone, Stan dialed a number he only had to use on a couple of previous occasions. Stan didn't trust nor like the man that he was calling. The General knew that for what he needed though, Doctor Mengel was also the only man for the job.

Stan Corbin sighed as the man he was thinking about answered the call. "Doctor Mengel here."

Stan closed his eyes, wishing he had another option. "Doctor Mengel, General Corbin here. We've had a problem at the Hidden Lake project and I'm going to need your help with a couple of witnesses."

On the other end of the line, the hazel eyes lit up as the Doctor ran one hand through his gray hair. "I'm sure that can be arranged. If you need my services, maybe you should tell me what has happened."

As Stan explained the situation and that he had not one but two patients that needed to be silenced, Karl Mengel's mind clicked into overdrive as he already began making plans.

As soon as he hung up the phone, Karl Mengel sat back in his chair and pressed his hands together in front of his chest, making them look like a steeple. The hazel eyes glittered as the gears in his mind began to spin.

Standing, Karl walked over to a large filing cabinet. The meticulous records he kept matched the overt cleanliness of his office. Pulling open one of the drawers, Karl flipped through the contents of the cabinet and then pulled out three files.

Returning to his desk, the Doctor slowly read through the information from the three files. Two of those files contained details from patients he had worked on. The third file was one that had been passed down to him from his father.

The Doctor Mengel, whose work Karl was looking at, was famous, or perhaps infamous would be a more appropriate description. That Doctor Mengel had been known for his borderline demented physical and psychological experiments. Of course, the first Doctor Mengel's research and trials were not the type a person could openly talk about. For Karl, that didn't matter, like his father, he would continue the work, even if it had to be done in a cloak of secrecy.

Luckily for him, there were people, like General Corbin, who always seemed to be in need of his services.

As he read through his father's files, Karl saw something interesting and stopped to peruse the file, a sadistic smile forming on his thin lips.

Chapter 8

As Seth and Andrea sat in the two chairs in their hospital room that were usually used by visitors, they were surprised when they looked up and saw General Corbin stepping into the room. They had both been expecting to see Doctor Paulson and hopefully with the results of their blood tests.

An older, extremely thin man with hazel eyes followed the General in.

Doctor Mengel had taken time before the two men had headed for the patients' room to explain his plans for Seth and Andrea to the General and what the ultimate result of their treatment would be. The General had accepted the plan wholeheartedly.

Something Mengel had never doubted the General would do.

Looking at the man that she had never seen before, Andrea didn't like the way the man's eyes seemed to look not at her, but instead directly into her. Although the man wore a Doctor's jacket, to Andrea it felt like he was anything but a Doctor. With that one stare she felt he had already examined her from the inside out. She had never met anyone who gave her the creeps like this stranger did, just by looking at not only her but Seth. Andrea felt a shiver run up her spine and as she turned to look at Seth, she saw he had the same look of repugnance on his face that her own must hold.

General Corbin stared at the two prisoners for just a moment, and then pointed toward the man who had already stepped toward the two. "This is Doctor Mengel, he's a specialist in toxic poisonings and he will be in charge of your care from now on."

Seth frowned, "Does Doctor Paulson know about this? He should be here any minute with our blood work results."

The General shook his head as a grin appeared on his face. "James Paulson will no longer be your Doctor, nor will he be allowed to help with your treatment. It will be Doctor Mengel who will be handling everything from now on. The Doctor prefers to work alone."

Karl Mengel nodded. "I've already looked at your tests and I have to inform you that I found both of you were exposed to toxins while you were at Hidden Lake. There's no need for either of you to worry. I have been treating cases like yours for many years and with great success I might add. We'll be starting both of you on medicine to counteract the poisons in your system."

Both Seth and Andrea stared at the Doctor like he was crazy. Seth stood up from his chair. "You can't do this. What if we refuse treatment?"

It was General Corbin who answered the question. "I'm afraid I can't allow you to refuse your treatment. We don't know yet if the two of you are contagious. I'm not going to let you out of this hospital and then end up with a catastrophe on my hands. If you don't willingly accept the treatment, you will be forced. I know that sounds harsh, but I've seen too many epidemics started by just one or two people who, like you, thought they were in good health."

Doctor Mengel nodded. "You may feel fine, but believe me, the tests are never wrong. You will both be having an IV started with the cure for the poison. You can remain here in the hospital. We should begin to see results within a day or two. At that time, we will run the blood tests again and see what kind of dent we've made in the toxic poisoning."

Andrea shook her head. "What about our families and our jobs. I need to call in sick to work."

The General stared at Andrea. "Don't worry about any of that. I'll make all the necessary calls. I have your information. I had to run background checks on your ID's. I'm sure you must see the predicament I am in. I needed to ensure you weren't up at Hidden Lake for the sole purpose of investigating the hazardous spill or even being part of it. In this time of terrorist problems, no one is to be trusted. What happened up at Hidden Lake, is being handled at this time through military channels. Until that is settled, I'm afraid you won't be allowed to make any phone calls. This situation is one that is best handled by experts. Now, the Doctor needs to begin his treatment. Are the two of you going to accept it willingly or do I need to bring in the guards?"

Seth turned to Andrea, who looked scared to death. "I don't think we have a choice right now. One way or another they'll make sure we get what they say is a cure."

Andrea sighed. "I don't like any of this. If we are being forced to accept treatment, I would like to know just what this so called cure entails. It's not something experimental you're going to be giving us is it?"

Doctor Mengel laughed lightly, the sound grating on Andrea's nerves. "You'll just be getting antibiotics along with some vitamins to strengthen your immune system. There's nothing to worry about."

The Doctors' words did nothing to reassure Seth or Andrea. They knew there was plenty to worry about and as of yet, neither had any clue as to how to get out of their predicament.

Doctor Mengel asked Seth and Andrea to return to their beds and then he excused himself to go out to the nurses' station to give orders for the starting of the IV's.

After he'd gone, General Corbin looked from one face to the other. "I know both of you are trying to make some kind of big conspiracy theory out of all this. Nothing even close to that is going on. In fact, in actuality, the story couldn't be further from that. The things you saw in that cave were actually items taken from a private collection. It was owned by a drug lord in the Middle East and nothing more. That man hurt a lot of people and is now in prison for life, exactly where he belongs. Hopefully we will be able to sort out who the treasure actually belongs to. Now, I better go and make some phone calls."

When the General left the room, Andrea stared at Seth, her face concerned. "You don't believe what he is saying do you? What if we're wrong about the treasure?"

Seth shook his head. "We're not wrong. Most of that stuff, including that necklace I found years ago, are old. I think the General is full of bullshit. Did you notice how he mentioned a drug lord in the Middle East as his scape goat? How cliché is that? I think he told us that story so we wouldn't continue to try and find the real secrets he's hiding. I still believe that treasure was stolen during World War Two by Hitler and the evil men who did his bidding."

Andrea nodded. "That's what I think too. If that treasure belonged to some Middle Eastern drug dealer and was recently obtained, I don't think it would be kept in a cave. It also doesn't explain that flying saucer we saw in the other cave."

Just then the door opened and a nurse came in with Doctor Mengel. Seth wondered if the woman worked for this hospital or for Mengel. He supposed at this point it didn't really matter.

While Doctor Mengel and the nurse were starting IV's on Seth and Andrea, General Corbin asked for and received the use of an empty office.

First he called the auto shop where Seth worked, easily getting the man who ran the shop to believe his concocted story.

Following that call, The General put in one to the factory where Andrea was employed. Using the toxic spill as a starting point, a fact the whole town of Hagen Falls, by now, had to be aware of, General Corbin was able to convince Andrea's employers also that she could be absent at least a week, probably two, for a medical leave of absence.

The next call was, unbeknownst to the general, a long distance call to Marta Vanussa, who was still visiting her sister in Michigan. General Corbin had gotten Marta's number from Andrea's cell phone and had naturally assumed the woman was in Hagen Falls. When the elderly woman answered, the General tried to make his voice firm, but compassionate.
"I'm trying to reach Marta Vanussa."

Marta's blue eyes frowned. "I'm Marta, who is this?"

The General spoke quickly. "Missus Vanussa, I am General Stan Corbin. I don't know a better way to tell you this than straight out. I'm afraid I have some bad news. Your granddaughter, Andrea Larson, was camping at Hidden Lake with Seth Reynolds. There was a chemical explosion at an operation there. I'm afraid both your granddaughter and Mister Reynolds were exposed to the toxins."

Marta's hand went to her heart. "Oh my goodness, that can't be, is she okay? Are they both okay?"

The General felt like laughing at how easily people were fooled. Instead he made his voice serious. "I'm sorry, but I'm afraid right now the news isn't good. Miss Larson and Mister Reynolds have been taken to the Veteran's Hospital in Monarch. Both of them have fallen into comas. The Doctors are doing all they can at this time. We won't know for a few days if the treatment the Doctors are trying will help or not. I really am sorry that I've had to share this tragedy over the phone."

As Marta's sister entered the room, Marta looked up at her with tears in her eyes. Ignoring her sister's curious look, Marta spoke to the General, her voice trembling. "Thank you for letting me know. I'll be on the next plane home."

Before the General could answer, the phone went dead.

Placing the receiver down, Stan Corbin smiled before picking it up again and dialing the number he had gotten from the cell phone he had taken from Seth's backpack for his parents.

As Sid Reynolds' answered the phone, General Corbin was careful to repeat the same made up story he had given to Marta Vanussa. The General had expected to receive the same response and wasn't disappointed as Sid's voice came over the line. "I just can't believe this is happening. How long are the two expected to be in comas? Isn't there anything that can be done?"

General Corbin was having a hard time keeping his voice sympathetic as he answered. "The Doctor and the hospital are doing all they can. I'm afraid, at the moment, all we can do is keep both your son and Miss Larson stable."

Sid felt like he'd been punched in the stomach. From where he sat in his kitchen, he could see his wife, Gwen, who was outside getting her gardens ready for winter, which was only a few months off. Right now, she was pulling the never endless collection of fallen leaves out of the garden bed.

Sid knew he needed to get off the phone and try to find a way to break the horrific news to his wife. A task he was dreading. Turning away from the window, Sid focused his attention back on the call. "Thanks for calling General, I need to let my wife and our sons know what's happened. As soon as we can we'll be at the hospital."

Hanging up the phone, Sid didn't walk outside immediately, but stayed sitting at the table, thinking about Seth. He loved all three of his sons, but being his first born, Seth would always hold a special place in his heart. When Sid had first found out Gwen had been expecting, just over thirty years ago, he had run to the store and picked up a miniature football and some toy cars and trucks. Sid had been sure from day one that Gwen was carrying a boy.

Gwen had laughed until tears had rolled from her eyes when her husband had come home bearing the presents. He had brought not only the toys for their yet to be born son, but a rose bush for her. She and Sid had gone straight to the backyard and planted the bush. Now the thing was over six feet high and three feet wide and covered with roses. It was also the spot where right now Gwen was standing and as Sid watched, busily pruning in the backyard.

Sid sighed and stood, knowing he couldn't procrastinate any longer.

Hearing the back door open, Gwen turned, the smile she had ready for her husband dissipating as she saw the look on Sid's face. Dropping her pruning shears, Gwen stepped over to hear what she already could already see was going to be devastating news. As a mother, her first thoughts were of her sons. "What's wrong Sid, who's hurt?"

Shaking his head, Sid placed both hands on his wife's slender shoulders. "It's Seth honey. Not just him either. From what I could understand, Seth and Andrea were up to the cabin and hiked down to Hidden Lake. They were exposed to that chemical spill up there that was in the paper. The two of them are in the VA Hospital in Monarch and they are in comas."

Hearing his wife's gasp, Sid moved his arms from her shoulders to slide around her waist and then helped her into the house. Once inside he assisted her to a chair at the table. Sid then sat down next to her and took her hands in his own. "We'll work this out Gwen. God knows this isn't the first trial we've had to go through. Let me call the boys. I know both Brady and Jarod will want to head to the hospital. Seth and Andrea are going to be okay. I won't believe any other way."

Nodding, Gwen gave her husband a smile. "I know, neither will I. Let me go change while you make the calls."

Gwen left the room as Sid picked up the phone. She waited until she was alone in the bedroom to break down and cry. Covering her face with her hands, Gwen let the tears fall as her sobs shook her shoulders.
It took ten minutes, but when she finally collected herself, Gwen changed clothes and then stepped in the bathroom and splashed

cold water on her face. Looking in the mirror, Gwen took several deep breaths, put on her brave face and then went back to the kitchen to let Sid know she was ready for the battle.

*

Back in the office, after he had hung up from that last call, Stan Corbin sighed as he sat back in his chair. He had done his job by passing on the word of the two patients' health to their families.

All he could do now was hope Mengel's experimental and probably highly unethical treatment worked quickly enough to put Seth and Andrea into the comas he had just told their families about and before their relatives arrived at the hospital.

General Stan Corbin hated putting faith in Karl Mengel, but at this point, he had no other choice. He couldn't let any information get out about what they were doing at not only Hidden Lake but at the other operations they had going all over the world. He had become part of the team twenty years ago and now he was too deeply embedded to allow the secrets out. Besides, he needed his share of the profits when the time came to sell the treasure to secret collectors. Stan Corbin wanted to get the hell out of not only the military, but the country.

Chapter 9

Sitting in the living room of her parents' house, Mel had just finished watching the morning news. The special news break that had interrupted the regular news was all about the closure of the Hidden Lake recreation area.

Although the news had been on before, Mel hadn't known about it. She hadn't watched the news while she was in the hospital and even now, no specific details were being given out. All Mel had been able to hear was scant information about the mysterious hazardous explosion and the subsequent toxic spill that had closed the recreation area. Everyone was being ordered to stay away from Hidden Lake. Mel hadn't heard from Seth or Andrea although she had tried to call both their cell phones repeatedly. The two hadn't actually said they were headed back to Seth's cabin, but Mel knew Seth's truck had been left up there when she'd had her accident and her friends had rushed her down to Hagen Falls to the hospital. She also knew something strange was happening up at Hidden Lake. If her friends had gone up there to get Seth's truck, Mel was also certain her best friends were now in trouble.

As she was thinking about that, her mom stepped into the room. One look at her mom's unusually pale face confirmed her thoughts even before Maria spoke. "Honey, Andrea's grandmother is on the phone. She needs to talk to you."

Mel hadn't even noticed the phone in her mom's hand until her mom handed it to her. Frowning and worried, Mel took the phone and spoke into it. "Hello, Missus Vanussa, this is Mel."

Marta sighed. "Melanie, thank goodness. Are you okay? How did you get away from the lake? Have you seen or heard from Andrea and Seth?"

Mel frowned. "Slow down, I think you lost me. I hurt my leg at the lake. I just got out of the hospital. Where are Andrea and Seth? I haven't seen either of them for a couple of days. I've been trying to call both of them and they don't answer their cell phones either."

Marta frowned. "I thought you knew. I assumed you were with them at the lake. I was actually calling your mom to see if she had any information when she put you on the line. Andrea and Seth are in the VA Hospital in Monarch. Both of them are in comas. I'm going to be flying home tonight."

Mel felt her heart drop. "Oh my gosh, what happened Missus Vanussa?"

Marta shook her head. "I hardly know anything. Some General called me and said Andrea and Seth were exposed to a hazardous spill up at Hidden Lake. Weren't you with them?"

Mel took a minute to explain about the camping trip and her breaking her leg. She didn't say anything about the cave or the spaceship. When she finished her story, Mel tried her best to comfort her best friend's grandmother. "I'll have my mom and dad drive me up there and see what I can find out. I'll call you as soon as I can."

Mel hung up the phone and repeated what she'd just learned to her mom. It didn't take long for Maria to get her husband Daniel and the three were on their way to Monarch and the Veteran's Hospital.

It took an hour to get there and another half an hour before they were allowed into the room where Seth and Andrea lay on their separate beds. Both looked like they were sleeping. The steady beat of their heart monitors was the only sound in the room as

Mel's father pushed her wheelchair through the doorway.

Just a short time before they were allowed to visit, General Corbin had discreetly removed Corporals Vaugn and Weston from outside the hospital room's door.

Once the General had made the calls to Seth and Andrea's families, he knew it wouldn't be long until they had visitors. Thankfully, Doctor Mengel's 'cure' of pentobarbital and whatever other chemicals the mad Doctor had concocted, had worked quickly and the Generals' made up story of both Seth's and Andrea's comas had become a reality.

Mel clamped her hands tightly on the arms of her wheelchair as she stared in disbelief at the scene before her. To see her best friends lying in the beds, as close to lifeless as possible, right in front of her, had to be the hardest thing she had ever done and was tearing Mel apart.

Maria, seeing the look on her daughter's face, placed her hand on Mel's back and gently rubbed small circles as she leaned down to whisper in Mel's ear. "It's okay honey, go talk to them. Your words will get through. Just talk to your friends and have faith sweetheart."

Mel nodded, but the lump that had appeared in her throat was so large, she wasn't sure she would be able to speak. Daniel Grayden pushed his daughter's wheelchair between the two beds that were close enough together Mel was able to reach her arms out to the sides and touch both Andrea and Seth's hands. For some reason, she had expected them to be cold. When she felt the warmth of their skin instead, it lifted Mel's spirits and she was able to talk. "I'm sorry I didn't get here sooner. I talked to your grandma Andrea. She's catching a plane and will be here tonight. I haven't talked to your family Seth, but I know they'll be here. I wish I knew what happened. Please, both of you need to fight. Come back to me. Seth, Andrea, if you can hear me, just keep fighting. I love you both and need you in my life. I promise to try and find out what happened. Please, don't give up."

Mel continued talking. Reminiscing about good times the three had shared until she heard the sound of someone stepping into the room. Both Mel and her parents turned at the intrusion.

The man standing in the doorway wore a Doctor's coat, but Mel saw none of the compassion in the hazel eyes that she associated with the Doctors she knew.

The man cleared his throat. "I'm sorry, but we have to keep visitations to a minimum at this time. You can of course come back tomorrow to visit. Until we see some type of improvement though, you will have to adhere to these rules."

Mel frowned. "Who are you?"

The man smiled, but it didn't touch his eyes. "I'm sorry, I should have introduced myself first. I'm Doctor Karl Mengel, I'm in charge here. Miss Larson and Mister Reynolds are under my care."

Mel's brown eyes narrowed. "If you are their Doctor, maybe you could tell us what's wrong with them. How in the world did any of this happen?"

The Doctor shook his head. "I'm afraid I don't know all the circumstances. From what I was told, there was an accident at Hidden Lake, toxic chemicals were spilled. These two were camping and were inadvertently exposed. When they were brought here, both were already comatose. We are doing all we can to reverse the damage. I can't tell you any more than that and like I said when I came in earlier, only short visits are allowed at this time. I'm sorry, but I am going to have to insist you end your visit for today."

Letting go of her friends' hands, Mel gripped the arms of her wheelchair until her knuckles turned white. She didn't like the idea of this man being in charge of her friends. For now though, she knew it would be better not to cause any trouble. She looked at her parents. "Let's go, we can come back tomorrow."

Daniel and Maria took their daughter out of the room. Neither of them felt any better than Mel did about the strange man in charge. Before they reached their SUV, Mel took the time to phone Marta and tried to explain the little she knew about Andrea and Seth and their condition. When she finished they went outside and Daniel loaded the wheelchair in his vehicle and they all began the drive back to Hagen Falls.

Mel, in the backseat, was trying to make a decision. Finally she nodded to herself as she made up her mind. "Mom, Dad, I need to tell you something. I'm not even sure how to explain what happened. First, I should tell you my accident didn't happen the way you were told. I'm sorry I didn't tell you the truth before. I did fall, but we weren't hiking at the time, we were running for our lives."

Maria turned in her seat to stare at her daughter. "Melanie, I think maybe you better explain this to us. Whatever happened we'll understand. I'm sure there's a good reason why you didn't tell us before. Just remember, we love you and like God, we also forgive."

Mel shook her head. "It's nothing like that. We didn't do anything wrong. All we wanted to do was explore a cave. You know the place where people see lights and a few have even claimed to see a spaceship up at Hidden Lake?"

Looking at her daughter, Maria nodded. Glancing in the rearview mirror at Mel, Daniel also nodded. "We're familiar with the place and the stories. What happened up there?"

Mel took a deep breath. "Seth took us to some tunnels that led to a cave. We were able to see into the cave from the tunnel. We saw a spaceship in there. It was my fault we were heard, I was the one who made the noise. The ship was being guarded by men with guns. I'm sure they were some kind of soldiers. We heard them shouting, saying not to let us escape. When we got out of the tunnel and were running, I tripped and fell. That's how I broke my leg." Mel shook her head, fighting the tears that were threatening. "I think Seth and Andrea went back up there to find out more. I don't believe what they are saying about the explosion and toxic spill. I don't know why they are hiding that they have a spaceship in that cave. I just know something strange is going on. I'm sorry I didn't tell you what really happened. Maybe if we had told you the truth to begin with, Andrea and Seth wouldn't have gone back up there and now they wouldn't be laying in that hospital." Mel's voice was shaky. "This is all my fault.

I feel like I have to do something. I don't like Seth and Andrea being taken care of by that man who calls himself a Doctor either. There's something really strange about that guy."

Maria nodded. "I got the same feeling from the man. Just being in the same room with him I feel like I need to go take a cleansing shower."

Daniel was also nodding at what his wife and daughter were saying, but then he frowned. "I'd like to see where this cave is and also that vessel you said was in that place. Right now they have the area up to Hidden Lake shut off though. We can't get up there."

Maria looked at her husband. "They can't keep it closed forever. Let's pray they end the closure soon. When they do, we are definitely headed up there. Mel's right, something strange is going on and I think both Andrea and Seth are in danger. I really have a strong feeling about that."

Mel frowned. "I know it is a bother, but I would really love to head to that hospital again to check on my friends. That creepy Doctor said we couldn't visit long today, but we could visit tomorrow. I can't drive with my damn leg in this cast. I know pushing me around in the wheelchair is a burden, but I would really appreciate if one of you could bring me up there." Melanie blew out a breath. "Oh hell, I really hate having this broken leg."

Maria smiled. "Don't worry, we'll take you up there and you are not a burden, never say that. Andrea and Seth are like family to us. Besides, I'd feel awful if we didn't check on them. I also know they'd do the same for you if you were in that place."

Melanie nodded. "They did more than that when they got me to the hospital after I fell." Melanie felt better knowing she would be going back, but she also couldn't stop the feeling of dread that settled over her.

Chapter 10

The next couple of days were hectic for Mel and she was sure even more so for her family. Even though neither of her parents had ever complained, she knew they had to give up a large part of each day to take her to the VA Hospital in Monarch. Besides the hour drive each way, there was the job of loading and unloading her wheelchair. Mel hated to ask for the help. She had always felt more comfortable as a giver not a receiver. She was used to being self-sufficient and was having a hard time in her new role as a patient and having to be dependent on others. She couldn't wait for the day she could get her cast off. Three months was going to be an eternity. She was hoping to get a walking cast put on within a few days and also hoping that would help her be a little more mobile and a lot more independent again.

As Mel's parents pulled into the VA hospital, Mel smiled and pointed. "Look, that's Seth's mom and dad."

Getting out from behind the wheel, Daniel hurried and took Mel's wheelchair out of the back of the SUV and then helped Mel get situated before pushing her over to where Sid and Gwen Reynolds were standing just outside the brick hospital's double front doors. Mel had talked to the Reynolds on the phone several times, but this was the first time she'd actually seen them in person since not only her accident, but also Seth and Andrea's tragedy.

The couple exchanged hugs with Mel and hellos with her parents. Gwen was shaking her head. "It looks like you really did a job on your leg."

Mel nodded. "I did, but lucky for me Seth and Andrea were there to take care of me

and then rush me to the hospital."
Saying her friends' names and thinking
about their predicament, Mel's voice
cracked with emotion. Taking a moment to
compose herself, Mel finally looked at
Gwen whose dark eyes were so like Seth's.
"Has there been any change?"

The head full of dark curls bent down as
Gwen sighed. She shook her head and as she
spoke, Mel could hear the weariness in the
woman's voice. "No sign of response in
either of them yet."

Sid put an arm around his wife's shoulders.
"It hasn't been that long yet Gwen. We just
have to have patience and hope."

Maria nodded. "Sid's right, I have a prayer
chain going at our church too."

Gwen smiled. "Thanks so much Maria."
Then she turned quickly to Mel. "Oh, by the
way, I forgot to tell you. Andrea's
grandmother is up there now. I know she'd
love to see everyone."

Mel smiled. "I can't wait to see her. I've been worried about her health too."

After good-byes all around, Mel and her parents headed to Seth and Andrea's room. As soon as they entered, a large smile lit up Marta's face. She stood from where she had been sitting next to Andrea's bed and hurried over to Mel.

Bending over the wheelchair, she hugged her granddaughters' best friend. "It's so good to see you. I'm so glad you're in that wheelchair and not laying in a bed. I mean, I'm not glad you got hurt, but, well, you know what I mean."

Mel sighed. "I feel so guilty Marta. I should have been with Seth and Andrea. I should be in one of these beds."

Marta shook her head of short gray hair. "I don't ever want to hear you say that again. I also know that Andrea and Seth would tell you the same thing and when they get better, I'm sure they will."

Mel smiled. "Thanks Marta, I don't know how true it is, but I really appreciate you feeling that way and saying that."

Marta moved away from Mel so she could be pushed between Seth and Andrea's beds. As the group visited in the hospital room, another visit was taking place in an office not far away.

General Corbin was standing in front of a seated Doctor Mengel. His face was covered with a dark scowl. "Damn it Mengel, what in the hell did you think you were doing? We've got two people in the comas you created and both have families visiting every damn day. If either of them wakes up even long enough to tell their tale we are in a hell of a mess. On the other hand, if they die, we'll most certainly have an investigation on our hands and more than likely a lawsuit. I don't think I have to tell you neither of these is an alternative I'll accept. Why in the hell didn't you just kill them the first day? I am holding you personally responsible."

The General's face was red from the exertion of yelling at the Doctor. Instead of screaming back a reply, Karl Mengel folded slender arms over his scrawny chest and leaned back in his chair. His face was serene, but the hazel eyes held hatred in their depths. "If you are done with your tirade, why don't you take a seat? First of all, you should remember you agreed to this solution. When I said I wanted to put Seth and Andrea in a comas, I had your approval. In fact, at the time, your ass was in a sling General. I solved your problem and kept your secret intact. Now it will be me who saves your sorry hide once again. I have the resolution to your problem. By tomorrow morning, everything will be taken care of without lawsuits or any secrets revealed by your prisoners."

General Corbin's blue eyes looked almost dark grey as they narrowed, but he took a seat. "Okay Mengel, let's hear this plan of yours. It better be good."

Karl Mengel smiled, a cold calculating grin, before he began to explain his plan. As he spoke, the look on Corbins' face echoed his own devious one and the General slowly nodded. "That might just work. How can you be sure they won't remember though?"

Mengel had a haughty expression on his face. "When I'm finished, you can question them if you want. It's really not necessary though. My solution will work."

Mengel leaned forward in his chair. "Shall I proceed with my plan?"

Looking at the arrogance on the Doctor's face, Stan Corbin wished he had other options. Knowing he didn't, the General slowly nodded. "Go ahead and do it, but you better be right. I can't afford anymore screw ups."

Mengel stood and walked out of the room, not bothering to give an answer to the General's last words.

*

After the busy day at the hospital had finally begun to wind down, and the darkness of night surrounded the building, Karl Mengel walked down the quiet hallway with a purposeful stride. The nurses who had been watching over Seth Reynolds and Andrea Larson had been given orders the two patients weren't to be bothered for the remainder of the night. Knowing Doctor Mengel would be sitting in the room, none of the staff cared to be anywhere near the hospital room.

As Doctor Mengel entered the room, he glared at the two patients. It was time to begin the work that would bring about his solution to General Corbins' problem.

Stepping over to the beds, Doctor Mengel decided to begin with Seth. Using a formula he had modified from one his father had created, Karl brought Seth out of the coma to a semi-conscious state. It only took a moment from that point for the Doctor to place Seth in a hypnotic trance.

Karl Mengel first traveled back in time with Seth. Regressing his patient, Karl examined Seth's life, going back to when Seth had first invited not only the woman who slept in the bed on the other side of him in the hospital room, but someone named Melanie, to his cabin. Karl was surprised to learn that not only had this person Melanie been with Seth and Andrea, but that all three of them had seen the ship in the cave. The only thing he could do about that memory was to keep it in Seth's mind. It would have been too much of a challenge and too risky to destroy that recollection in the chance that Melanie would bring it up at a later date. If he did erase that happening, Mengel knew he would have to find this Melanie person and erase her memory also. Instead, Karl moved on to when Seth and Andrea had gone back to the caves and overheard the guards. He tweaked that memory slightly and then began the process of erasing all memories of not only the hidden treasure, but the way that had Seth had found the documentary that led him and Andrea to that cave that held the treasures to begin with. Karl wondered what General Corbin would think about that documentary. He knew he should tell the General what he had learned, but almost felt like not sharing the information and letting the man dig himself out of that predicament. He pushed the thought aside for when he had more time to decide what path to take on that idea. Karl kept working, erasing all memory of the pairs' capture and their first visit to the hospital. When the memories were vanquished, Karl let out a deep breath and then pulling a small notebook from his coat pocket, Karl worked methodically as he inserted the new memories he had jotted down into Seth's brain. When he finished, the doctor gave Seth the command to sleep until he received the new command that would allow him to wake.

Karl then repeated the procedure with Andrea, careful to make her memories at Hidden Lake match Seth's. He placed them at the cabin, doing mundane things and then instead of a trip to the tunnels where they found the treasure, the two went on the hike that led them to the accidental spill where they were exposed to the toxic chemicals. The same poisons that had put both of them in the comas they were in now.
When he had finished, Karl also told Andrea it was time to sleep.

Mengel then sat back in his chair to wait. All that was left for him to do now was command the pair to wake in the morning. When they did, the only things they would remember would be what he had told them to with hypnotic suggestions.
Karl set the alarm on his phone. He wanted to be awake, done with his work and far from the room before any of the nurses

showed up for the morning shift.

Waking up before the alarm. Karl went to work. Sitting between the beds, Karl spoke to both his patients. "Seth and Andrea, when I count to ten, you'll awaken. At that time, you will be able to remember your uneventful camping trip. You will be drowsy for a day, but then your health will return. Nod if you understand me."

Waiting for the slight nods, the Doctor then counted to ten. His eyes moved from side to side as his attention went back and forth between Seth and Andrea. Grinning, he watched as the two pairs of eyelids fluttered several times before they finally opened.

Matching frowns appeared on the faces Karl was watching. He reached out so he could touch Seth and Andrea on their arms. "Just relax, you're in the hospital. You were exposed to toxic chemicals at Hidden Lake, but both of you are going to be okay. I'm Doctor Mengel and you've been under my care for a few days now. You were both in a coma, from your exposure, but everything is going to be fine now."

Andrea stared at the man. There was something in the hazel eyes she didn't like. Unable to pinpoint the feeling or the reasoning behind it, she pulled her gaze away and looked at Seth. She tried to say something, but her throat and lips were so dry they felt like they were cracking.

Looking at Andrea, Seth licked his own dry, chapped lips. "Morning."
The word was spoken in a quivering whisper, the sound hoarse.

Mengel stood. "Let me go get you some ice chips. You've both been given IV's to keep you hydrated but that doesn't help that dry mouth much. I'll be right back."

Leaving the room, Mengel went to the nurses' station and ordered Misty, who was the nurse on duty, to deliver ice chips to the

225

newly awakened patients. The green eyes widened. "You mean they're awake? That's terrific, what an amazing way to start the day."

Doctor Mengel grinned his manipulative smile. He though it passed as a normal look, but he was the only one who believed that way. "It is good news. I'd say our hard work has paid off."

Misty didn't think anyone had done anything special, instead she felt it was more a combination of time and numerous prayers that had brought the two back from their slumber. She knew better than to mention her ideas to Mengel. Instead she hurried off to go and get the ice chips and then headed to the hospital room where the patients waited.

Stepping in the door, Misty smiled brightly. "Well, it's about time you two sleeping beauties woke up."

Misty spoon fed a sliver of ice to Andrea and then did the same for Seth. "This is such a miracle. We hadn't noticed a change in either of your conditions. It works that way with comas sometimes though. It doesn't really matter, I'm just so glad to see you both awake. "

Misty looked at the monitors next to both beds. The screens displayed blood pressure, pulse and oxygen saturation for both patients. The readings for both patients was well within the normal range. Misty pointed at the screens. "All your signs look good. I bet you both are hungry. Why don't I go see if we can get you some food? It might be an all liquid breakfast though."

Seth smiled, feeling better after the ice chips. "Personally, I'll take what I can get." The voice was gravelly, but music to Misty and Andrea's ears.

Andrea laughed lightly, feeling the roughness in her own throat.

"That's my Seth." She turned to Misty. "I'd be happy with a cup of coffee."

Misty nodded. "I'll see what I can do. I'll call your families too. It'll be a pleasure to give them some good news."

When Misty left the room, Andrea and Seth stared at each other for a long time before Andrea frowned. "What happened Seth? I remember camping and then taking a hike around the lake, but how'd we get here? That Doctor said we've both been in a coma."

Seth was quiet a moment as he racked his brain for memories and finally a picture formed. "There were men by the lake. I think they were military."

Andrea gasped and nodded. "That's right, it was some kind of accident, a chemical spill like the Doctor said."

Seth frowned. "Seeing those soldiers or whoever they were is the last thing I remember."

Andrea nodded. "Me too, we must have been exposed to the chemicals and then passed out or something. Those men must have brought us here." Andrea sighed. "They saved our lives." The words were said in amazed wonder.

Seth nodded. "Thank God they were there."

Both Seth and Andrea were quiet then as they contemplated their good luck.

*

Down the hall, Doctor Mengel was filling General Corbin in on the details of the mission he'd just accomplished.

The General was skeptical and as soon as he was able to get away from Mengel, Stan headed to Seth and Andrea's room to start his interrogation of the two. He would have rather stayed out of the spotlight, now that the two had no memories of him, but he knew his presence would be expected because of the nature of Seth and Andrea's supposed toxic exposure. He also had to make sure for his own piece of mind that Mengel's treatment had worked.

An hour later, Stan Corbin left the room assured that Mengel had done what he had said he would. All the answers Corbin received from Seth and Andrea showed the false memories Mengel had given them had indeed replaced the real ones. General Corbin was satisfied his secrets were safe.

After the General left Andrea and Seth alone in the room, Andrea turned to face Seth, her forehead creased with worry. "What do you think that was all about? Doesn't it seem strange that the General was so concerned about our camping trip? I felt like he was interrogating us."

Seth nodded. "I got that feeling myself. It's funny how well our stories matched."

Andrea shrugged. "I guess because it was just you and me up there. It would make sense for us to tell the same story."

Seth shook his head. "It's more than that. When you were answering his questions, the same answers popped into my mind and almost word for word. Our whole trip feels a bit out-of-focus to me, but when that General asked about what we did, I just seemed to somehow find the answers. It's funny though, we both said we spent time playing cards." Seth closed his eyes drumming up a picture, he could see the two of them sitting at the table in the cabin with cards in their hands, but that was as far as the memory went. Seth opened his eyes. "I do remember us playing, but I can't remember what the game was or any other details."

As Andrea realized that what Seth was saying was almost the same thing that had been going on in her own mind, she felt like she had stopped breathing. Andrea took several breaths to make sure that hadn't happened. "Do you think this is some kind of strange side effect from those poisons they said we were exposed to or from our time in comas?"

Seth shrugged. "I don't know Andrea, but when that Doctor comes back, I'm going to have a few questions to ask him."

Letting out a breath, Andrea nodded. "I'm glad you're here with me Seth. I'm sorry we both had to go through what we did, but of anyone I know, you're the one I feel safe with and want by my inside."

Seth smiled. "I feel the same way."

As Seth stared at Andrea, touched by her words, she opened her mouth and yawned. Seth laughed at the surprised look on her face. "Yeah, I'm tired too, but I'm almost afraid to go to sleep."

Thinking of the comas they both had just come out of, Andrea sighed. "I know exactly what you mean."

Despite their worries, that should have kept them wide awake, Seth felt his eyes growing heavy, on the bed next to him, Andrea was having the same problem and the two were both fast asleep within minutes.

Andrea was the first to wake when she felt a light touch on her arm. Opening her eyes, Andrea turned her head and then smiled at the sight of her grandma's lovely face. Sitting next to her granddaughters' bed, Marta couldn't help the tears that moistened her eyes. "They said you both had come out of your slumber. I've been sitting here afraid to try to wake you, in case they were wrong." Marta stood and hugged Andrea. "It's so good to have you back."

A voice from the next bed had Marta smiling. "Hey, what about me?"

Marta walked over and hugged Seth. "I'm just happy to see both of you awake." Looking from Seth to Andrea, Marta smiled. "It's a double miracle. Never doubt the power of prayer. We've all been praying for you to wake up and Maria Grayden has even had a large prayer chain going for both of you."

As Seth listened to Marta. He glanced over at the door and beamed as his parents and his brothers walked in. The couples' broad smiles almost matched Seth's. The two brother's also had wide smiles for not only Seth but Andrea. It was Andrea who spoke to them first though. "Hi, I'm so glad you're all here, now we just need Mel and her parents' to drop by and complete the group. I can't wait to see Mel and to tell her Mom thanks for keeping the prayers going."

Gwen and Sid Reynolds walked over to their son's bed, but Gwen turned to Andrea. "I talked to Melanie. She said to tell you her parents would bring her by later this evening."

After Gwen and Sid grabbed their son in a hug, they stepped over and repeated the action with Andrea. Brady and Jarod did the same before taking chairs in the room.

The small group settled down then and had been visiting almost an hour when Doctor Mengel stepped into the room, and looked at Seth and Andrea. "I'm so glad to see your families are here. Nothing is better for a smooth and quick recovery than good family and friends. I'm afraid though it would be best to keep all visits to a minimum, at least for today. The nurses will be coming in soon and I think it's about time to get you two some food. Why don't I let you say your good-byes for today? I'll go and let the nurses know it will be okay for them to come in."

When Mengel left Andrea shook her head in disgust. "Even if that man is the one responsible for our recovery, I still can't make myself like him." Andrea shuddered. "There's just something strange about him."

No one in the room disagreed with Andrea's statement. Mostly because all of them harbored the same feelings about Doctor Mengel.

Instead of dwelling on the negativity surrounding Mengel, Seth and Andrea's relatives focused on many hugs and saying their good-byes with promises to visit again as soon as possible.

Not long after they left, a nurse came in to check both Andrea and Seth's vital statistics and to draw some blood from the pair. She also promised to make sure the two would be brought lunch trays before she left the room.

Doctor Mengel stepped in shortly after the nurse had gone. Looking at Seth and Andrea, he grinned, but the gesture looked more like a grimace to the rooms' occupants. "I have to say, the two of you are looking much better. We should be able to get your test results back later today or by morning at the latest. If the toxins are gone, we can see about getting the two of you released. I'm sure that both of you are more than ready to go home."

Andrea nodded, but Seth frowned. "We're ready to get out of here, but we'd also like a few questions answered."

Frowning, Doctor Mengel pulled over a chair and sat so he was at the foot of Seth's bed. "What do you want to know? I'm sorry, I can't really disclose too much about your recovery because the source of the toxin hasn't been discovered. Any information has to be kept secret until the government along with the military probes further into their investigation."

Shaking his head, Seth frowned. "I don't care about who created that toxic mess up at Hidden Lake. What I want to know is why

Andrea and I are having such a hard time remembering any details of the past few days. I mean the time just before we ended up in this hospital and in comas. We both remember camping, but nothing seems clear. We seem to have the same story in our minds with little deviance in the answers we give when questioned about it."

The doctor shook his head. "I don't know about why your answers seem to match, I think that is probably just a coincidence. As for your memories, they will be obscured, of course. You have to remember you both were exposed to extremely powerful toxins and the coma you have both been in will make your brain unclear. I can't guarantee it, but I feel those memories will begin to become more distinguishable as time passes. I'm afraid that, although hard, you both are just going to have to have a lot of patience."

The Doctor was saved from answering any more questions when a nurse pushed in a cart with Andrea and Seth's lunches on it.

"Looks like your food is here. I'll try to get back later to check on you. If I don't get back tonight, I promise I will be here first thing in the morning and hopefully see about getting the two of you out of here."

Seth's face was covered in irritation as he watched the Doctor walk out. He didn't think the Doctor had come up with what conceivably could be called a reasonable explanation to his and Andrea's problems. Seth also had to wonder if that was on purpose.

After the two had finished their meal, they were both given massages and some light exercise for muscles that seemed to have lost their elasticity during their sleep. It seemed hardly any time had passed before yet another nurse came in their room to see what they would like for dinner.

Waiting for the meal, Seth turned to stare at Andrea. It was the first time since Mengel had left that the two had gotten much time alone. "What do you think about what the Doctor said?"

Andrea shrugged. "His explanations sound almost like our descriptions of what happened to us. It felt to me like he read them out of a text book somewhere."

Seth nodded. "Yeah, if it is a spy text book. The information has to be kept secret. What the hell kind of explanation is that?"

Frowning, Andrea shook her head. "I don't even want to think about all that, right now, all I want is to get out of this place and get home. Nothing here feels real or right."

Seth tried to smile, but his heart wasn't really in the half grin he gave Andrea. "You're right, maybe once we get out of here, our memories will actually straighten up. I might just be trying to make too much of the situation."

Andrea nodded, but in her heart she was sure Seth wasn't doing that. In fact, she wondered if they both weren't up against something unfathomable.

After their evening meal, Seth and Andrea found an old movie to watch on the hospital's television. The few channels they found, didn't have a very big selection to choose from. Before the movie had gotten half way done, the pair turned from the television screen when they heard an excited squeal from the doorway. "Look at you two, wide awake. I can't believe it."

Mel moved as fast as her wheelchair would allow over to Andrea's bed and hugged her and then placed a kiss on her cheek. "I'm so happy you're okay. You look great."

Andrea smiled, but Seth grunted. "Hey, I look great too don't I?"

Moving around Andrea's bed, Mel made her way over to where Seth lay on his. Bending down she planted a slobbery kiss on his cheek. "You look amazing. Much better than before."

Wiping the wetness of his cheek, Seth frowned. "I happen to know I look good when I am sleeping, just like a baby."

Mel laughed. "Hey, don't get me wrong, you're a real sleeping beauty, but I like you much better with your eyes wide open." Mel turned to Andrea. "That goes for you too."

Andrea smiled. "Thanks, I like us better with our eyes open too. Thanks for coming by. Where's your mom and dad?"

Mel smiled. "Oh, they'll be right up. My mom saw that creepy Doctor Mengel that's been taking care of the two of you and is letting him know that her prayers had more to do with both of you waking up then his medical expertise."

Andrea laughed. "Good for Maria. I happen to agree with her."

A musical laugh came from the doorway. "Good to hear you say that Andrea. I don't know if Doctor Mengel agrees. I don't really

care what that man thinks though. I know
the real reason behind the miracles that
happened here."

Maria stepped over and hugged Andrea and
then went over and hugged Seth. Daniel
followed behind his wife. "Maria's right, I
don't think too much of that guy. Although
he did say you two might be getting out of
here soon and that's about the only thing I
wanted to hear from him."

Both Seth and Andrea nodded at Daniel's
words. Mel and her family stayed less than
an hour seeing that Seth and Andrea both
still looked tired. Mel kissed both her friends
again and then reluctantly let her family take
her home. She knew she wouldn't feel better
until both her friends were out of the
hospital and back home.

*

The next morning after both Andrea and
Seth had finished their breakfasts, Doctor
Mengel stepped into their room. "I have

good news for both of you. The toxins in your body have been neutralized. Looks like tomorrow the two of you will be able to go home. I'd let you go today, but I think you need a bit more exercise. I'm going to have a physical therapist walk you around the hospital. We don't want to let you out until you're physical ready. You've both been in a prone position for a while and need to get your bodies used to walking. I think once you get home you both need to still take it easy and I would like you to check back with me or with your family Doctor in Hagen Falls in a week or two. If you get a clean bill of health then, I don't see any reason why you can't return to all the activities that encompassed your normal lives before all of this happened."

Dr. Mengel nodded to himself, satisfied with his proclamation and then quickly left the room.

Seth rolled his eyes. "I know one thing, if I have to see a Doctor for a check-up, it definitely won't be that guy."

Andrea nodded emphatically. "That goes double for me. There really is something wrong with that guy. I think I'd really love to see a Doctor in Hagen Falls though. I'd like to see what they think about our poisoning or whatever it was."

Seth nodded. "Except Mengel's not giving out any information. How in the hell would they know what to check for to begin with?"

Andrea stared at Seth. "I never even thought about that. I guess we just have a check-up and see if anything shows up. I just can't wait until tomorrow, so we can get out of this place."

Chapter 11

Standing outside the hospital, Mel couldn't help the beaming smile that graced her face. It was a great day. She'd just been given her walking cast and now Seth and Andrea were being released and with a bill of good health.

Mels' dad had gone inside the hospital to pick up her two friends. Daniel had readily agreed to take all of them up to Seth's cabin to collect the vehicles that had been left there. Maria hadn't been able to get away, much to her disappointment, to join them. Although Mel had the walking cast and a new set of crutches, she'd decided not to attempt the long walk into the hospital.

As the front doors of the hospital opened, Mel waved at her dad and at her two friends who followed him. The two carried the backpacks that they had worn when they were first brought to the hospital. A memory that neither Seth nor Andrea had left.

All three waved back and hurried over to Mel. Seth and Andrea gave her hugs, made awkward by Mel's crutches. Andrea smiled. "Look at you, standing on your own."

Mel shrugged. "Well, almost. Hopefully I won't be on the crutches too long either. I can't wait until I have no cast at all."
She looked from Andrea to Seth. "Never mind about me, you both look great. I'm so glad you're getting out of this place."

Seth laughed. "Tell me about it."
He turned to Daniel. "I really appreciate your taking us to the cabin."

The man, who was a total opposite in looks from his daughter, smiled as he ran a hand through his blonde hair. "I'm happy to do it. If everyone wants to get in, we can get away from this place."

Seth and Andrea got in the backseat with Andrea seated behind Mel. The seat Mel was in was pushed back as far as it would go to make room for her cast.

As soon as everyone was settled, Daniel drove away from the hospital and headed for the cabin at Hidden Lake.

On the drive up, Mel turned to look at Seth. "You two never did tell me if you found out anything more about that spaceship when you both came back up here."

Seth frowned. "I almost forgot about that. In fact my brain is a little fuzzy. It feels like years since we saw that thing."

Andrea nodded. "I feel the same way. It's like I woke from a dream and nothing from the time Mel drove us up to meet Seth at his cabin really happened."

Mel frowned. "You've both been through a lot. I can't believe you didn't think about that ship though. I didn't want to ask about it until you were out of the hospital, but that's all that's been on my mind." Mel then sighed. "I'm so sorry about all you had to deal with. But what about that spaceship?"

Seth shook his head. "It turned out to not be an actual spaceship. When Andrea and I came back up here, we snuck into the tunnels behind the cave. We overheard the guards talking. The damn thing is a prototype the military was working on."

Daniel frowned. "Why in the hell did they hide it up in that cave?"

Seth shook his head. "I guess they figured they could keep it a secret there. It seems Hidden Lake wasn't remote enough though. I've heard a lot of stories of people thinking they saw a U.F.O."

Mel laughed. "Yeah, including me. What a letdown. I really wanted to show it to my dad."

Seth looked at Mel. "We can still show him. We can drive almost up to that cave and from there we can help you walk the rest of the way."

Mel smiled. "Don't worry about me, I would crawl if I had to. I'm more worried about you and Andrea. Are you both up to walking?"

Seth nodded. "After laying in that bed, I'm just glad to be out and moving."

Andrea laughed. "Me too, I feel like we laid in that place for years instead of days."

Daniel nodded. "Okay we go to the cave then. In the paper and on the news they said, the military contained that spill and have left the area. According to both sources they are still looking for whoever was behind the whole explosion though. There shouldn't be any guards to worry about now anyway."

Mel smiled. "Can we go there before we go to your cabin?"

Seth shrugged. "It's okay by me."

As Daniel drove, Seth gave him directions, guiding from the back seat until they drove as far as they could go. Seth pointed at a hill about two blocks ahead of them. "That's where the cave is. We'll have to walk from here."

Getting out of the vehicle, Seth and Daniel got on either side of Mel to help her if she needed it. Andrea walked on the other side of Seth. The four slowly made their way to the cave. Even though Daniel said the military people had left the area, Seth was still surprised when no guards were there to stop them as they stepped into the cave.

For Andrea, the feeling was more of relief than surprise. She had been afraid they would be seen and thrown back in the hospital again. Either that or exposed to chemicals over again. She definitely didn't want that to happen and found herself taking shallow breaths. Then feeling ridiculous, she resumed normal breathing.

Seth pointed ahead of them at the cave. "That's the place where we saw the ship." The group moved more quickly and then entered cautiously into the large cavern entrance. As they stepped in, the four looked around the spacious, but clearly empty area, knowing now why the military presence had left.

Mel was the first to speak, her tone filled with dismay. "It's gone, why would they take that spaceship out of here?"

Daniel shrugged. "Maybe they didn't want any more witnesses to what they were working on. They'll claim it was never here. It's your word against theirs' about what you saw and none of you have any proof."

Seth looked up at the cave ceiling and frowned at the rock above him. "That was different before, remember, it was a normal ceiling, not rock, and looked like it slid open."

Andrea shook her head. "I didn't see it."

Mel stared at Seth. "Neither did I. When that guard turned to look at the place we were hiding, I was too busy just trying to get away from there."

Seth's face turned into a scowl. "It was there, I don't know how they covered it up, but I know damn well what I saw."

Daniel stared at the three who had been through so much and sighed. "For what it's worth, I believe you three and what you say you saw. What bothers me is that they moved it. If it is a new technology we're capable of, why hide it from the public?"

Mel nodded. "It also makes me wonder if it wasn't moved because that prototype spaceship was actually based on a genuine ship from space."

Everyone in the room was quiet contemplating what Mel had just said. Seeing the dejected look on the three faces, Daniel shook his head. "C'mon, let's get out of here and get over to Seth's cabin."

The small group left the cave and headed back to the SUV and then drove to the cabin. Seth smiled as Daniel pulled in and parked next to the two vehicles sitting there.

"Hey, at least my truck and Andrea's car are here. I was beginning to think the whole thing really was a dream."

Andrea nodded. "I had that feeling myself."

Seth and Andrea went in the cabin to make sure everything was okay. Andrea grabbed the bags she and Mel had left from the bedroom. The ones she hadn't retrieved when just she and Seth had come back up to the cabin. Seth locked up the cabin before they walked over to where the others waited. He looked at Daniel. "Why don't you take the lead? Andrea can drive behind you and

I'll be right behind her. All I want to do is get home and put all this behind me."

Andrea nodded. "That and I can't wait to soak in a hot bath. I'm sick of hospital showers."

Daniel nodded. "Sounds good to me, but don't forget that Maria is having a dinner for both of you tonight. She expects the two of you to be there at six."

Seth and Andrea both said they'd be there. The truth was they couldn't wait to have some of Maria's home cooking.

Two hours later, Mel and Daniel were at home, Andrea was soaking in the tub at her place and Seth was sitting in his living room. He was trying to figure out not only why the military had moved that ship, but how they had accomplished the feat of changing the cave ceiling to look just like any other cave. He knew he had seen a place for an opening in that ceiling. He also knew it would bother him until he got the chance to go back up there, preferably with a ladder, so he could get an up close look at the ceiling of the cave.

Seth sighed and leaned back on the couch, glad to be home. Looking at the coffee table in front of him, Seth frowned. Then he reached a hand out and picked up the object that had caught his attention. Lifting the necklace, Seth let it dangle from his fingers. He didn't remember bringing the necklace out here. He always kept it in the bedroom. Seth closed his eyes as he tried to draw up a memory and an answer to why he had put the necklace on his coffee table. When nothing materialized, Seth opened his eyes and frowned, as he berated himself for not being able to find a reason. His mind had been foggy since he'd woken that morning in the hospital to see Doctor Mengel sitting between the bed he lay on and the one Andrea occupied. Although Mengel had told him and Andrea that having the memories mixed up and hard to capture was normal and would eventually go away he wasn't so sure. Seth really hoped the Doctor was right. He'd always prided himself on having a fairly sharp mind and he didn't like the feeling of his brain being in a fog.

Seth shook his head and reached for his laptop. He had e-mails to check and also a Facebook and Twitter account he needed to look at. He wasn't an avid participant on Social Media, but he usually checked in every few days. As he opened his laptop, Seth was going to check his e-mails, when he decided to look instead at his recent searches, hoping that would somehow refresh his lagging memory.

Frowning at the last search he had done, Seth clicked on the link and his world turned upside down.

Chapter 12

It took all the determination and patience
Seth had to not place a call to Andrea or
Mel. He decided instead to wait until
Maria's dinner when he could talk to
everyone face to face.

After arriving at the dinner, Seth looked at
everyone enjoying themselves and knew it
would be better to wait until they'd all eaten
before broaching the subject of what may or
may not have happened to him and Andrea.

Seth picked at his meal, hoping no one
noticed his unusual lack of appetite.
After dinner, the table was cleared and
Maria brought out cake and coffee for
everyone. As she handed Seth his, she
frowned at the man who was like another
son to her. "Seth, are you okay? You hardly

ate anything. Well, for you that is. Usually you have seconds or thirds. It looked to me like you barely finished your first serving."

Sighing, Seth nodded realizing now that his lack of large appetite hadn't gone unnoticed. Then shook he his head. "To tell you the truth, I'm not sure if I'm okay or not."

Everyone around the table stared at Seth, waiting for him to explain. Looking at each face, Seth's gaze made it around the table before he looked down, studying his hands as he tried to sort through what was on his mind. Finally, he lifted his head and looked at Andrea. "You said before that you felt like the time from when you and Mel drove to the cabin until we woke up in the hospital was a like a dream."

Andrea nodded, but frowned, not understanding where Seth was going. "I do feel that way. It's really hard to explain. My mind just feels funny. It reminds me of looking at something through a semitransparent window, the kind like you might see in a bathroom. You know what you're seeing, but it's a bit distorted from the actual thing."

Seth nodded. "Exactly and looking back, the memories feel strange to me too. I don't know quite how to explain it either, maybe they just feel a little too perfect to be real."

Everyone around the table stared at Seth, wondering what this was all about.
Seth, seeing he was the focus of curious attention, shrugged. "It all started when I got home earlier. I found a gold necklace sitting out on my coffee table in my living room. It was one I found years ago up near Hidden Lake."

Mel nodded. "I remember you telling Andrea and me about it."

Seth nodded. "But did I actually show it to either of you?"

When the two shook their heads, Seth continued. "I wouldn't have taken that necklace out except to show it to someone. I have no memory of doing that."

Seth wasn't sure how to share the rest of his story. Finally he decided to just be honest and tell them everything he had found on his laptop. "After I saw that necklace, and couldn't remember ever bringing it out and placing it there, I decided to check my laptop for the internet searches I did before all of this happened. I was hoping something, anything, would jog my memories. As I opened the link, I didn't remember ever seeing that last search I found on my computer. It was a site about treasures stolen during World War Two and hidden around the world. According to the documentary that was included, Hitler and his Nazi party were able to collect vast amounts of treasure during the time they ruled the country. I should say they stole it, not collected it, because that's what they did." Seth shook his head in disgust. "They got away with not only that, but so many other appalling things before their evil was finally stopped. According to this documentary the treasure they had pilfered, was ordered by Hitler to be moved and hidden in various locations around the world. From what I could gather from the documentary, the Nazi party planned on using that treasure much later to expand their empire and be able to live like Kings while doing it."

When Seth finished talking, everyone but Andrea stared wide eyed at him.

Andrea instead, was now the one who was staring at her hands like she found them fascinating. Not actually looking at her hands, Andrea was instead thinking how this story of Seth's seemed more real to her than any recollections she'd been having of the two of them up camping up at his cabin. When Andrea looked up, her blue eyes fastened on Seth's brown eyes. "I think I saw that documentary and I don't think it was very long ago. What in the hell is going on Seth?"

Her friend shook his head. "I don't know, but whatever really happened up at Hidden Lake, we have no way to prove it."

Mel drew in a breath. "Just like that spaceship in the cave."

Now it was Maria's turn to shake her head in disgust. She'd been devastated when she'd been told about the group finding nothing but an empty cave earlier. "I've always felt the Government or the Military were hiding secrets up at that place." She turned to Seth. "Did that documentary mention Hidden Lake or this area as a possible hiding place for the Nazi's stolen treasures?"

Seth shook his head. "No, but the places they mentioned were similar to Hidden Lake in location and scenery."

Everyone around the table was silent a moment, wondering what could be done with the information they might have uncovered, and apparently for the second time for Andrea and Seth.

It was Daniel who broke the silence. "I'd like to get the names of the people who made that documentary. Maybe we could find a way to reach them and get some answers."

Seth smiled at Daniel. "That sounds like a great idea, thanks. I've been going over this whole situation in my head and that's the first idea that sounds plausible."

Daniel smiled. "Maybe you were just trying too hard. Sometimes, you have to be on the outside looking in to find the right answer. You know, just think of me as a sort of objective observer."

The feeling in the room lightened as they thought about Daniel's idea. At least it gave the group a direction to take and Seth laughed, turning to Maria. "You know what? I think I'd like another piece of cake now."

Maria stood up. "Now that is good to hear. It was a little bit scary seeing you not eating."

Everyone had to agree with Maria as they talked of other things until the time came for Seth and Andrea to head home.

Both of them had the feeling that they'd made a breakthrough and had a chance to straighten out the mess that they were now positive false memories had somehow made.

Chapter 13

Both Seth and Andrea returned to work just two days after their, what they were told was, a miraculous recovery.

For Seth, there was something comforting about returning to the job he loved. Andrea, on the other hand, was feeling more overwhelmed than anything. It wasn't the work at the factory so much as it was the surroundings that she found herself in. Without Mel by her side, Andrea realized just how much she hated the job. Even when Mel had been working next to her, the mind numbing job had been tedious. Now, every time she looked up from her work, she could see the people who had been staring at her, dipping their heads, trying not to be noticed.

She'd already answered the same questions dozens of times in her first week back. She didn't mind the inquiries into Mel's health, but the retelling of her own story was getting old. Especially considering the fact she wasn't even sure what exactly had happened to her and Seth while they had been up at Hidden Lake.

Even to her own ears, the recollections of camping, the accident and then ending up in a coma alongside Seth sounded like a practiced explanation. Thinking back on her time, to her, was like seeing images in a thick fog and then trying to explain what they looked like without having a clear picture.

Trying to ignore the furtive looks of her co-workers, Andrea tried to stay focused on her work.

By the time her first break had come, Andrea decided she'd had enough. Walking directly to the human resources office, she knocked on the door.

When she heard Maggie Porter yell 'come in', Andrea took a deep breath and grabbing the knob tightly, turned it and stepped into the woman's office. Andrea had worked at the factory almost three years and she could only remember seeing Maggie Porter a handful of occasions during that time.

The woman looked up when Andrea stepped in, a puzzled look on her face before she squinted at the name tag Andrea wore. "Is there something I can do for you Andrea?"

Reaching a hand to her chest, Andrea nodded as she pulled off her name badge and then the apron that was considered her uniform.

Placing both on Maggie's' already cluttered desk, a slight smile crossed Andrea's face. She brushed her light brown hair back from her forehead. "Yes, I quit."

A scowl replaced the curious look that had been on Maggie Porter's face. "What do you mean you quit? Are you trying to tell me you are putting in your two weeks' notice?"

Andrea shook her head. "No, I'm not. I'm letting you know I am done here, starting right now."

Maggie thumped a finger on the apron that lay in front of her. "I think you should reconsider doing that. Bayden Plastics happens to be the best paying job not only in Hagen Falls, but in the whole state. Without notice, there will be no chance of your being rehired and that would also mean you will not be given a good recommendation from us to any future employers. Maybe we could discuss your problems and we could come up with a different solution."

Andrea couldn't help but laugh. "You know what, I don't want to discuss my problems and I don't really care to be rehired and don't need your endorsement to a future employer. I'm done here and that's all there is to it."

Andrea turned and walked from the room and out of the building she had spent the last three years working in. As she stepped out into the cold, brisk fall air, Andrea felt rejuvenated.

As she drove from the factory to the nearest drive through coffee shop, Andrea was trying to calculate how long she could survive before she had to find another job. Her small house was paid for by a trust fund her parents had left to her. She had planned on selling it and looking for a newer, maybe slightly larger place. Instead of that, she could take part of the money she'd been saving for a different house and use it to pay off her car loan. With both house and car paid for and if she was thrifty, Andrea thought the remaining balance in her savings account would see her through a year of unemployment.

As Andrea pulled up to the window at the coffee shop, she ordered two Mocha Cappuccinos. She couldn't wait to deliver one to Mel, along with the news of being jobless.

Placing the coffees in the car's cup holder, Andrea felt a twinge of guilt at her indulgence, but decided to call it a gift to herself in celebration of her new found freedom, then she pulled away from the coffee shop and headed to Mel's parents' house.

When Andrea pulled in, she was glad to see an empty driveway. She loved Mel's parents, but wanted to explain all of this just to Mel for now.

After Andrea knocked on the door, she stood shifting from foot to foot as she waited for Mel. She knew it would take her friend a few minutes to make it to the door, even with the walking cast.

When Mel finally made her way to the door and opened it, she was surprised to see Andrea standing there. "Andrea, what's wrong, why aren't you at work?"

Holding up the coffees, Andrea shrugged. "If you have a minute, we can drink these and I'll try and explain."

Mel opened the door wider. "Come on in, all I seem to have lately is time on my hands. Let's go in the kitchen and you can tell me what kind of trouble you've gotten yourself into now."

Walking in the kitchen, Andrea placed the drinks on the table and then took a seat. Mel took the one opposite, sitting so her leg, in its' cast, was sticking out and away from the table. Mel reached forward and grabbed one of the cups. "Thanks for the coffee. Now, tell me what in the hell is going on."

Andrea lifted her shoulders. "Not much, I just walked off the job. You're the first person I thought of to share the good news with."

Mel stared wide eyed at her friend. "What happened? You've been down there for what, almost three years now?"

Andrea nodded. "Almost as long as you. I think I started a few months after you did."

Mel shook her head. "Wow, I can't believe this. I mean, I know that job sucks, but it is good money. What are you going to do now?"

Shaking her head, Andrea stared at her friend. "To tell you the truth, I haven't had time to give it a whole lot of thought, but I'm thinking of just taking some time off from any work for a while."

Mel nodded. "It sounds like a great idea, but can you afford that?"

Andrea nodded. "I think I can survive at least a year. Then I can have time to find a job I actually like."

Mel smiled. "Good timing, I'll be on medical leave at least a few more months."

Andrea grinned. "We can keep each other out of trouble. You know what, you should give up your rental and move in with me. I mean, you won't be staying at your parents' house too much longer. No sense in paying rent. My house is small, but it does have two bedrooms and two bathrooms."

Nodding enthusiastically, Mel smiled. "That sounds like a terrific idea. I want to pay you rent though. I'm still getting paid a partial wage while this damn leg heals and I can get physically be ready to go back to work."

Andrea nodded. "Good, it looks like we're going to be roommates then. Hey, maybe quitting that job will be the best thing I've ever done."

Mel nodded as she picked up her coffee and waited for Andrea to pick hers up so they could put their cups together in a toast. "Here's to new beginnings."

Smiling, Andrea nodded. "I can't wait to tell Seth."

Laughing, Mel shook her head. "I bet it's the last thing he'll be expecting to hear. Let's head over there later. He usually gets off around five or six."

Andrea nodded. "Great idea, I need to head home and get some stuff done. Why don't I drop back around five thirty or so and pick you up. We can share the news with him together."

Mel nodded and started to get up, but Andrea stopped her. "Just stay there, you don't need to walk me out."

As Mel smiled thankfully, Andrea grabbed her coffee and left the house and then drove to her own place.

Sitting in her driveway, Andrea tried to look at her house objectively. The first words that came to mind were cute or maybe charming. The light gray house with its' turquoise trim had always made Andrea think of a cottage from a fairy tale. The yard was small in front with a few bushes on either side of the front porch. In the back it was larger and had an enormous apple tree in the center. Andrea had bought a picnic table years ago and put it under the tree. It was great in the summer to have a shady place to sit and relax, usually with Mel and Seth by her side. The place didn't have a garage, but the alley in the back of her place gave room for extra vehicle parking. Maybe she and Mel could get one of those portable carports for winter. Andrea smiled broadly, thinking that this new chapter in her life was going to bring only good things.

Getting out of the car, Andrea headed inside. She wasn't sure when Mel would be moving in, but decided since she had the rest of the day, and maybe a year, off, she might as well get busy getting things ready for her new tenant. Andrea spent the remainder of the day cleaning out the spare bedroom and its' adjoining bath. Wondering the whole time why she hadn't asked Melanie to move in with her before. Andrea didn't want to ask Mel to pay rent, but it would be great to have someone help out with the other expenses, like utilities and food.

Andrea was glad that her and Mel we're going over to Seth's. She'd talked to him on the phone since the dinner at Mel's parents' house, but he hadn't said anything about finding the person or people responsible for the documentary. Now that she wasn't working, she might have time to help Seth with the search of the makers if he needed it.

Taking a break after she finished her cleaning, Andrea put on some coffee and sat at her kitchen table while she waited for the pot to brew. Andrea fingered the necklace she always wore as she waited. It was a habit she didn't want to get rid of. Rubbing the necklace always made her think of her parents. She did that now, wondering what they would think of the recent turn of events her life had taken. Frowning, Andrea took off the unique necklace her parents had made and left to their only daughter. Opening the locket, Andrea stared at the picture inside. Her parents' smiling faces looked back at her. At the time the picture was taken, her parents had to be close in age to her now twenty seven. Andrea sighed thinking the picture must have been taken not long before their untimely deaths.

Closing the locket, Andrea studied it more closely. Her parents had both been talented artists, the jewelry they produced one of a kind, and from what Andrea had been told by her grandparents, highly sought after. Andrea had never really tried anything artistic and wondered now if her parents' talents had been passed down to her. She decided it would definitely be worth a chance of finding out. Smiling, Andrea wondered if maybe she had just decided her future vocation.

Looking at her watch, Andrea decided she still had time for a quick visit with her grandma before she had to pick up Mel. After finishing her cup of coffee, Andrea drove to her grandma's.

After visiting with her grandma a few moments, catching up on things, Andrea broke the news about her new jobless situation. As soon as she let her grandma digest the information she broached the idea she had of following in her parents' footsteps and becoming a jewelry designer.

Marta smiled. "That's wonderful, they would be so proud. I still have some of their jewelry making supplies out in the shed. That stuff rightfully belongs to you anyway."

Andrea couldn't believe how everything seemed to be falling into place. "That's so great grandma. I'll come back in a day or two and have a look. I'm sorry to cut our visit short, but I need to head over and pick up Mel. We're going to head to Seth's and share all that's happened today with him."

Andrea stood and hugged her grandmother. "I'll see you in a few days."

Leaving her grandma, Andrea headed over to Mel's parents' house where she had to take time to explain to them about not only quitting her job, but her hopes for a new career, before she and Mel were able to get away and head for Seth's place.

Seth smiled broadly when he opened the door. "Well, what do you know? My two favorite people in the world. Come on in. I was actually just getting ready to call you both. I have some interesting news to share with you."

As Andrea and Mel both broke out laughing, because they too had interesting news to share, Seth frowned. "What's so funny? What have the two of you been up to?"

As they walked through the door, the two headed past Seth into the living room and sat down before Andrea took the time to explain about quitting her job. Then she told Seth her idea for trying to make jewelry.

Seth shook his head, astonished at all that had happened. "Sounds like you've had quite the day."

Andrea nodded. "Oh, wait, there's even more. Mel's going to give up her apartment and moving into my place."

Mel smiled and nodded. "Maybe I can even help you with your jewelry business. Then I won't have to go back to that horrible factory either. I mean once I get this cast off and I'm back on my feet."

Andrea smiled, her blue eyes sparkling. "I'd love that Mel." She turned to Seth. "You said you had your own interesting news to share. What's going on with you Seth?"

Looking at the two women, Seth shrugged. "Actually, it isn't just about me, my news involves all of us." Seth had to smile at the curious looks on his friends' faces. He thought about taking his time and leaving the two in suspense, but he couldn't help himself from sharing the news. "I found the man who produced the documentary about the hidden treasures and the conspiracy behind them."

At first Andrea and Mel were speechless, then both asked the same question, their voices mingling into one. "Who is he?"

Seth laughed. "His name is Jacob Steinman. He's agreed to share with us all that he and a group he works with, know about the hidden treasures. Most of what he's told me are the same things I saw on the documentary, but he has promised to keep in touch and share what they uncover. It's hard for him to find time to spare. From what I've learned so far, Jacob and the others travel all over the world in search of places like Hidden Lake and are working on several more documentaries."

Andrea looked at Seth, her blue eyes shining. "That's amazing news Seth. I know I saw that documentary before, but I really can't remember much about it. Do you think we could all watch it?"

Mel nodded. "I'd really love to see it."

Reaching for his laptop, Seth nodded. "Sure, I should have had both of you watch it before or at least give you the link so you could watch it yourself. Both of you come and sit next to me and we can all watch it."

Joining Seth on the couch, Andrea and Mel stared in speechless amazement as the documentary they were watching told the horrific story that was unfortunately still happening. It was one thing to have Seth tell them what he had seen and another to watch it unfold for themselves.

*

The next few weeks were busy for the trio. Seth continued to keep in touch with Jacob Steinman, both by phone and e-mail. For Andrea and Mel the days were filled with learning how to make jewelry and trying to turn that knowledge into a business. Andrea was finding, much to her delight, she did have artistic talents, passed on from her parents. She was glad to use those abilities to build an inventory of unique jewelry.

Mel helped with some of the designing, but found her real passion was in the organizing and managing of the business. She had already found several buyers for the works Andrea had produced. Now the two had to focus on putting together brochures of the jewelry and the setting up of an online business for the products. Mel had found many of the buyers were interested in specialized, one of a kind pieces that, because of their rarity, also would be bringing in a big profit.

Several times, not only Andrea and Mel, but Seth also, mentioned the coincidence that Andrea and Mel were making heirlooms not unlike those stolen and hidden during the horrors of World War Two.

Andrea liked to think the treasures she made would indeed become heirlooms, like the locket, she always wore, and that they would be passed down, hopefully with heartwarming memories from family member to family member.

It was those same types of items, Jacob Steinman and the group he represented were now busy trying to expose to the world and possibly return to their rightful owners.

Chapter 14

It had taken six months of e-mails and phone calls, but finally Seth, Andrea and Mel were meeting with Jacob Steinman, Jacob was the producer of the documentary that had started Seth and Andrea on the search for hidden treasure and left them with what they now knew were false memories.

The two had agreed that Mel should be included in the meeting. Although she hadn't been with them on the second part of their mysterious adventure, she had been with them when it had begun. When the three of them had first found the spaceship in the cave. Besides, she was their friend and they wanted her with them.

Seth knocked on the office door in the building they had been given the address to.

It had taken six hours to get here, using Mel's car, which had more room. Even though Mel had her cast removed and could now drive, she had been happy to let Seth take the driver's seat.

As the door opened, Seth was surprised to see a man who looked to be around sixty years old and who had a thick head of white hair standing in front of him Although Seth had talked to Jacob Steinman on the phone and exchanged numerous e-mails, he'd never actually seen the man's picture. To Seth, the image he had in his mind was of a man at least twenty years younger.

Jacob smiled. "You must be Seth."

Nodding, Seth pointed at the two women with him. "I am and these are my friends, Andrea and Mel."

Jacob shook all their hands. "It's so good to meet all of you. Seth has told me your story so many times, I feel as if I actually lived through it myself."

Jacob pointed toward a table in the room. "Come in and sit down. I have coffee ready and also some doughnuts."

Both Mel and Andrea turned to look at Seth at the mention of doughnuts. Seth stared back. "Hey, you two don't have to look at me like that."

Andrea laughed and turned to Jacob. "Seth has a reputation for a large appetite."

Jacob smiled. "I'm that way myself. Just go on over and help yourself. I have plenty."

Andrea looked at Jacob's well-built frame and thought he and Seth must share the same metabolism if Jacob really meant what he said about having a large appetite.

After everyone got their coffee and doughnuts, they took their seats with Jacob sitting at the head of the table. The eyes looking at the group were a light blue and reminded Andrea of the late actor, Paul Newman, whose eyes she had always loved.

They were the kind of eyes that gave you a sense of honesty and trust. Already she felt Jacob was someone she liked.

Taking a drink of his coffee, Jacob used the time to gather his thoughts. Setting down the cup, Jacob began talking. "I don't know how much Seth has told you two about what I am involved in. I think I should give you a background as to why I am so interested in this project first. My father, God rest his soul, was a holocaust survivor. He didn't marry and start a family until after he escaped from the death camps and moved to America. When I was old enough to understand, I was told the horrific stories of what he and others endured. The tales of survival were amazing." Jacob looked at the three sitting at the table. "I'm sure you've all heard some like them. My father's story is really no different than that of countless others, too many others. He lived through that hell and somehow was able to keep his dignity intact. The only bitterness he couldn't seem to let go of, was knowing the awful people, who killed millions, also stole heirlooms and treasures from those not only in the camps, but from their nation. For some people, their only connection to family was a piece of gold jewelry handed down through generations. The Nazi's had everything and yet, they still wanted more. They stole those people's hopes by taking their small treasures. My father always believed by the time Hitler and his Nazi party were finished, they had collected a vast treasure. He also believed it should be found and given back to the rightful owners, their ancestors or a museum that was able to tell their stories through those stolen treasures."

Jacob stopped talking long enough to wet his dry throat with a drink of coffee before continuing. "At the time of the holocaust, everyone had heard rumors of Hitler's orders to move that treasure out of Germany and to hide it in several isolated locations. I think his goal was to someday build resorts for himself and his followers near each treasure and why he picked locations with beautiful landscapes. I didn't have Hidden Lake on my list of possible sites, but it does fit the descriptions of all the others. I believe that Seth and Andrea saw a treasure and I know the military and the government would do anything and I mean anything to stop that story from coming out. I've talked to several therapists, without giving out your true identities, and they believe you were brain washed using hypnosis to strip your real memories and replace them with false ones. Those same therapists also tell me that they can help you regain those true memories that were stolen from you like the treasures were stolen from those people."

Andrea gave Jacob a sad smile. "I know in my heart I saw the treasure. The memories I have now, though lacking detail, are of simple times spent camping with Seth. I think I'll keep them over the real ones. I don't think I want to know what was done or who was behind it."

Seth nodded. "I feel the same way Andrea does, but I would love to see that treasure and others like it back where they belong."

Mel nodded. "I would too. I didn't have my memories stolen, but what those people did, what they've been doing since World War Two…" Mel shook her head. "The world has a right to know."

Jacob nodded and now his blue eyes had a sparkle to them. "The world will know. There's a large organization of people who feel the way you three do. They won't stop hunting and researching until the secrets are all exposed and the treasure returned. You should know, we have added the area around Hidden Lake to our investigations. I don't think that treasure was moved too far from the caves where you saw the spaceship. We'll find it, I promise you that. Although it might help our investigation to know who did this to you, I understand your decision not to have those memories returned. We're almost certain who is behind it anyway and we have the names you gave us of Doctor Mengel and General Corbin. Their names, along with a few others keep surfacing. We are definitely watching those people. It may take a couple of years before we have enough evidence to try and convict those involved. In the meantime, the documentaries will continue. Each time one is shown, more and more people come forward, like you three have done. Patience and perseverance is something the organization has plenty of. I thank you, and I know the others do, for your courage telling your story."

Seth frowned. "If it would help, I'd have this therapy you're talking about."

Andrea was about to say she'd be willing to do the same when Jacob shook his head. "I wouldn't ask that of either of you. I'm touched by the offer though. All I ask of the three of you is to go make new memories. If along the way, you find people who are open minded enough to listen, tell them the conspiracy. When the time comes for us to hold these people accountable for their atrocities, it will help if what they did is already on the publics' mind."

Jacob finished his coffee, glad to have his long speech over. Andrea was smiling at the man. "Thanks for what you're doing Jacob and I'm sorry for what your father went through."

Mel nodded. "I feel the same as Andrea, you are a remarkable man."

Jacob shook his head. "Those who made it through the holocaust are the remarkable ones. It is for them I am doing this, and like the others, won't stop until the job is completed."

Jacob stood and went to a desk at the far side of the room. He returned with six DVD's. He handed two each to the three friends. "These are the other documentaries we have been working on. I hope they will help you understand a bit more about the past atrocities and how we will be trying to rectify the appalling things done in the future."

After visiting a little more with Jacob, the three friends stood and now exchanged hugs and thanks with the extraordinary man before they left his office and headed home.

Chapter 15

Andrea and Mel had gotten their new business 'Dreams to Treasures' going on-line and we're now busy trying to find a house that also could be used as a home business to set up their jewelry shop. Business was going well and both were glad for the reprieve in the form of a weekend invite to spend time with Seth at his cabin.

Right now, Seth, Andrea and Mel were sitting on the deck of Seth's cabin looking out at Hidden Lake. This was the first time the three had come back up here since they had returned that day and found the cave had been emptied out.

Spring was out in full force and Andrea was gazing toward the far side of the lake. Although the scenery was breathtaking, Andrea's attention wasn't actually focused on the spectacular beauty that surrounded the lake. Or maybe she was, but not so much on the present location, as on the past that had been so rudely brought to life by the conspiracy done years ago and that Jacob and his group had uncovered. A conspiracy that now her and her two best friends couldn't help but be involved in.

Mel watched her, frowning at the melancholy look in her friend's eyes. "Are you okay Andrea? You look so sad."

Turning to look at Mel, Andrea nodded. "I was just thinking. This place is so beautiful. All the trees and bushes with their brilliant flowers reflected on the lake. Hitler picked places like this to hide his stolen treasure. Do you think a man who did the horrific things he did, had a part somewhere deep inside him that could appreciate beauty?"

Mel shrugged. "I don't know Andrea, I suppose even the most evil person has something good in them somewhere."

Seth looked at the two women, thinking about their conversation. "I've heard that without evil, there would be no way for us to recognize good. Maybe because of all his evil, Hitler was in need of something good and beautiful. I have to admit though, I'm glad the bastard didn't live and come here to see this beautiful place or to be allowed to enjoy any of the treasures he stole."

Mel and Andrea looked at their friend. Seth lifted one side of his mouth in a half smile. "I hope that doesn't sound harsh."

Andrea shook her head. "Not to me it doesn't."

Mel also shook her head. "Me either, I just hope Jacob can expose the story and return the treasure."

Mel stared at her friends. "The world needs to know what happened and remember that horrific time and maybe, just maybe, that knowing will prevent that kind of terrible tragedy from ever happening again."

Both Seth and Andrea nodded in agreement and hoped that their friend was right.

Thanks so much for reading. I hope you enjoyed the journey. You might have noticed, I am fascinated by conspiracy theories like the one in the book. I have written a lot of novels with different conspiracies as a backdrop to the story.

You never know when you or I might find ourselves in the center of one. My hope, is that when I do, I have good friends and family to stand by me, as together we figure a way out.

The same is true of all aspects of life and I want to thank amazing family and friends who have stood by me and encouraged me in this journey I call writing and I hope you call an adventure worth reading.

P.S. Winn

Novels

Foretold
Voices
Obligations
Tunnels
Capernicious
B.A. 47
Pacific Passage
Suppression
Lies in Shadows
Phases
Mystic Valley
The New Moon Killer
Healings
Superstition Canyon
Collisions
Viewings
Parallel Adventures - Into the Caves
Parallel Adventures - Secrets Revealed
A Gradual Decline
Judgments

Collections

Visitations
Heartfelts
Stretched Stories
Stretched Stories 2

Comic books

The Golden Years
The Golden Years 2

For Children

The Alphabet Book
The Number Book
The Secret Life of Goats
No, Jimmy, No

The books can be found on Amazon and
Barnes & Noble